I0434915

Georgia's

Forests, 2004

Richard A. Harper, Nathan D. McClure, Tony G. Johnson,
J. Frank Green, James K. Johnson, David B. Dickinson,
James L. Chamberlain, KaDonna C. Randolph, and Sonja N. Oswalt

United States
Department of
Agriculture

Forest Service

Southern
Research Station

Resource Bulletin
SRS–149

Richard A. Harper is a Forester and Forest Resource Analyst with the U.S. Department of Agriculture Forest Service, Southern Research Station, Forest Inventory and Analysis Research Work Unit, Knoxville, TN 37919.

Nathan D. McClure is the Director, Forest Products Utilization, Marketing, and Development Program, Georgia Forestry Commission, Macon, GA 31202–0819.

Tony G. Johnson is a Supervisory Forester with the U.S. Department of Agriculture Forest Service, Southern Research Station, Forest Inventory and Analysis Research Work Unit, Knoxville, TN 37919.

J. Frank Green is the Interim Chief of Forest Management, Georgia Forestry Commission, Macon, GA 31202–0819.

James K. Johnson is the Forest Health Coordinator, Georgia Forestry Commission, Macon, GA 31202–0819.

David B. Dickinson is the Forest Inventory and Analysis State Coordinator, Georgia Forestry Commission, Macon, GA 31202–0819.

James L. Chamberlain is a Research Forest Products Technologist with the U.S. Department of Agriculture Forest Service, Southern Research Station, Tree Buffer Technologies for Sustainable Land Use Research Work Unit, Blacksburg, VA 24060.

KaDonna C. Randolph is a Research Forester with the U.S. Department of Agriculture Forest Service, Southern Research Station, Forest Inventory and Analysis Research Work Unit, Knoxville, TN 37919.

Sonja N. Oswalt is a Forester and Forest Resource Analyst with the U.S. Department of Agriculture Forest Service, Southern Research Station, Forest Inventory and Analysis Research Work Unit, Knoxville, TN 37919.

Pine stand in south Georgia. (photo courtesy of the Georgia Forestry Commission)

Georgia's
Forests, 2004

Richard A. Harper, Nathan D. McClure, Tony G. Johnson,
J. Frank Green, James K. Johnson, David B. Dickinson,
James L. Chamberlain, KaDonna C. Randolph, and Sonja N. Oswalt

Fall colors. (photo courtesy of the Georgia Forestry Commission)

Robert Farris

Jimmy L. Reaves

A stable land base with sustainable forest resources is now—and will always be—vital to every Georgian. For more than 50 years, Georgia's forested area has been stable at about 24.7 million acres, even as our population and resulting development have increased. Tree inventory volume is currently at an all-time high for both softwood and hardwood. Tree growth exceeds total tree volume removed for both softwood and hardwood. Through a concerted effort by forest landowners, the forestry community, and policymakers, Georgia's forests are on the road to sustainability.

Since the 1930s, the U.S. Forest Service has tracked changes in the composition, extent, and condition of the forest land in Georgia through the Forest Inventory and Analysis (FIA) Program. The results of these inventories have been used for strategic planning and to make informed decisions by policymakers, foresters, landowners, loggers, industry producers, and researchers.

In 1997, Georgia was the first State organization to begin a partnership with the Forest Service to conduct the forest inventory. The partnership between the Georgia Forestry Commission and the Forest Service, Southern Research Station, FIA Program has strengthened data collection, resulting in more timely data output and the expansion of the inventory to cover all lands of the State.

This report displays the results of the eighth forest inventory of Georgia. It presents the current status of the timber resource through area and volume data, incorporating information about timber production and its socioeconomic importance. The impact of recent human induced and natural disturbances, changing ownership, and land use on forest health is also described.

It is with great pride that the Georgia Forestry Commission and Forest Service present this report about the status of Georgia's forests. We view ours as a relationship that will continue to grow, enabling us to provide the most accurate and useful information about the forest resources of Georgia—now and in the future.

Robert Farris
Director,
Georgia Forestry Commission

Jimmy L. Reaves
Director, Southern Research Station,
U.S. Forest Service

Foreword

This resource bulletin describes the principal findings of the eighth inventory of Georgia's forest resources. Data on the extent, condition, and classification of forest land and associated timber volumes, growth, removals, and mortality are described and interpreted.

In order to provide more frequent and nationally consistent information on the forest resources of the United States, the change from periodic to annual surveys was mandated by the Agriculture Research Extension and Education Reform Act of 1998 (Farm Bill). These surveys are part of a continuing nationwide undertaking by the regional experiment stations of the Forest Service, U.S. Department of Agriculture. Inventories of the 13 Southern States (Alabama, Arkansas, Florida, Georgia, Kentucky, Louisiana, Mississippi, North Carolina, Oklahoma, South Carolina, Tennessee, Texas, and Virginia) and the Commonwealth of Puerto Rico are conducted by the Southern Research Station, Forest Inventory and Analysis (FIA) Research Work Unit operating from its headquarters in Knoxville, TN, with offices in Asheville, NC, and Starkville, MS.

The primary objective of these surveys is to inventory and evaluate all forest and related resources annually. These multiresource data help provide a basis for formulating forest policies and programs and for the orderly development and use of the resources. The information presented is applicable at the State and unit level; it furnishes the background for intensive studies of critical situations but is not designed to reflect conditions at very small scales. More information about Forest Service resource inventories is available in "Forest Service Resource Inventories: An Overview" (U.S. Department of Agriculture Forest Service 1992). More detailed information about new sampling methodologies employed in annual FIA inventories can be found in "The Enhanced Forest Inventory and Analysis Program— National Sampling Design and Estimation Procedures" (Bechtold and Patterson 2005).

Field work began in January 1998 and was completed in September 2004. Seven previous surveys, completed in 1936, 1953, 1961, 1972, 1982, 1989, and 1997 provide statistics for measuring changes and trends over the past 68 years. This report primarily emphasizes changes and trends in recent years and their implication for Georgia's forests.

Tabular data for the FIA reports are designed to provide a comprehensive array of forest resource statistics. The 35 core tables that complement this report can be downloaded from http://srsfia2. fs.fed.us/states/Georgia. Additional data is available to those that require more specialized information for Southern States can be accessed directly via the Internet at: http://srsfia2.fs.fed.us/. Data in a format common to the two FIA units in the Eastern United States are also available. These data may be obtained from the Internet site referenced above.

Additional information about any aspect of this survey may be obtained from:

Forest Inventory and Analysis
Southern Research Station
4700 Old Kingston Pike
Knoxville, TN 37919
Telephone: 865-862-2000

Acknowledgments

The Southern Research Station gratefully acknowledges the cooperation and excellent assistance provided by the Georgia Forestry Commission in the collection of field data. The research was made possible through the collaboration of Forest Service, FIA personnel (including those in Data Collection, Information Management, Analysis, and Publication Management). Brett Butler from the Northern Research Station provided data tables from the National Woodland Owner Survey. Appreciation is also expressed for the cooperation of other public agencies and private landowners in providing access to measurement plots.

The following people were responsible for collection of field data:

FIA Staff

Robert Claybrook
Jeremy Rogers
Greg Smith

Georgia Forestry Commission Staff

Ryan Adamczak
Brian Allen
Charles Bailey
Jeremy Banks
Chris Barnes
Daniel Bender
Phil Broome
Brent Bryant
Paul Carson
Dan Chappell
Troy Clymer
Chad David
Ben Dickerson
David Dickinson
(Current GFC Coordinator and former GFC Field)
Chris Dowdy
Arnold Dyer
Jason Gillis
Kent Johnson
Thomas Marbut
Mark McClellan
Babe McGowan
Keith Moss
Tony Page (Former GFC Coordinator)
Ben Parsons
Dru Preston
Chad Pritchett
Jeff Sibley
Tim Smarr
Chad Sutton
Scott Thackston
Larry Thompson
(Former GFC Coordinator)
Jack Tribble

Contents

Contents

Ginseng.
(SRS photo)

Text Figures

Page

Immature great blue herons.
(photo by Bill Leal)

Forests provide clean water habitats and family fishing. (SRS photo) and (inset) Redbreast bream. (photo courtesy of the Georgia Department of Natural Resources)

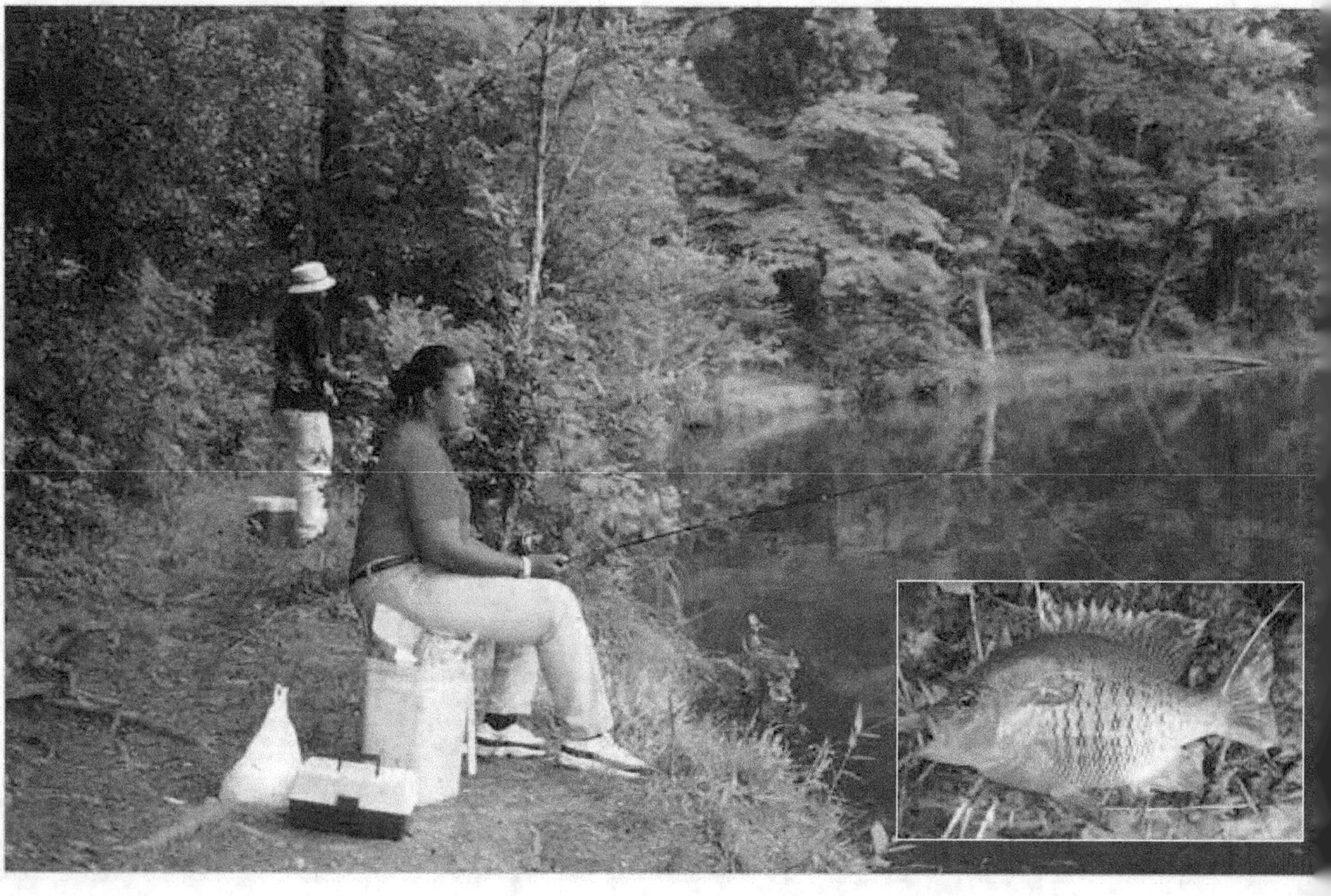

Page

Text Tables

Appendix Tables

Note: The 35 core tables that complement this report can be downloaded from http://srsfia2.fs.fed.us/states/Georgia.

Mature pine stand. (photo courtesy of the Georgia Forestry Commission)

Area

• Georgia contains the largest forest land area of all the States in the South with 24.8 million acres. Forested land covers about two-thirds of the State's 37.1 million acres.

• Timberland accounts for 65 percent of Georgia's land area and increased 450,000 acres to 24.2 million acres.

• Planted pine stands increased almost 7 percent since 1997 and totaled 6.5 million acres. Natural pine stands decreased almost 7 percent and totaled 4.3 million acres.

• Despite what seems to be favoritism for southern yellow pine, all hardwood forest types accounted for 55 percent of the timberland area with 13.2 million acres.

• Family forest accounted for 14.3 million acres, while forest industry and corporate owners accounted for 4.3 and 3.8 million acres, respectively. Public lands totaled 1.8 million acres.

Volume

• Softwood volume for all live trees reached an all-time high of 17.7 billion cubic feet and increased 16 percent since 1997.

• Hardwood volume for live trees increased 3 percent to an all-time high of 18.9 billion cubic feet since 1997.

• Loblolly pine added 2.0 billion cubic feet and totaled 9.9 billion cubic feet, or 56 percent of the softwood inventory in 2004. Longleaf pine volume increased 17 percent, its first increase in volume (and area) in decades.

• Volume for all live trees in pine plantations rose sharply marking a 45-percent increase to 6.7 billion cubic feet since 1997.

Net Growth and Removals

• For the period 1997 to 2004, the statewide average net annual growth for softwood live trees was 1.4 billion cubic feet, while removals averaged < 1.2 billion cubic feet. Net growth exceeded removals by more than 21 percent. This is an exceptional reversal compared to the 1997 and 1989 surveys when softwood removals exceeded net growth by 6 and 18 percent, respectively.

• Statewide, the average net annual growth for hardwood live trees was almost 625 million cubic feet, while removals averaged < 454 million cubic feet. For the last two surveys, i.e., 1989 and 1997, hardwood net growth exceeded removals by 26 and 38 percent, respectively.

• Average annual mortality declined since reported in 1997, with softwood mortality down 5 percent and hardwood down 12 percent.

Disturbance

• Final harvests averaged about 430,000 acres each year between 1997 and 2004 and accounted for < 1.8 percent of all timberland area.

• Some form of harvesting or timber stand improvement occurred on almost 860,000 acres annually or 3.5 percent of all timberland.

• Natural disturbances by category, i.e., fire, insects, and diseases, each represent < 1 percent of the total timberland area annually.

Load of logs being secured before hauling to the mill. (photo courtesy of the Georgia Forestry Commission)

Bedding—a form of site preparation for tree planting. (photo courtesy of the Georgia Forestry Commission)

Timber Product Output

• There were 181 primary wood-using mills in 2005 representing a decline of 120 mills during the last 20 years. However, production of roundwood increased about 1 percent since 1986.

• Average output during the 2004 survey was almost 1.6 billion cubic feet. This was a 4-percent decline since the 1997 survey.

• Softwood products accounted for 79 percent of the total output volume.

• Pulpwood was the leading product, accounting for 47 percent of the total output from Georgia's timberland.

• Saw logs were the second leading product accounting for 32 percent of the total output.

• Composite panel edged out veneer accounting for almost 7 percent compared to 5 percent. The remaining industrial output accounted for 4 percent while fuelwood accounted for 5 percent.

Economic Impact

• In 2006, the forest industry (nurseries, logging, and primary and secondary manufacturing) accounted for $17.8 billion in total revenue and employed 67,733 individuals with an annual compensation of $3.5 billion.

• The total economic activity accounted for more than $27.7 billion and employed almost 149,000 people who received annual compensation of $6.8 billion.

• Tax revenues generated from forest industry contributed $580 million to the Georgia State budget. An estimated $180 million of this tax went to provide for government services (such as education).

• Forest industry ranks second in employee compensation and third in number of employees among industries in Georgia in 2006.

• Major revenues from nontimber forest products (NTFP) came from Christmas trees and pine straw which contributed an average of $9.2 million and $26.5 million to the Georgia economy from 2001 to 2005.

Merchandizing logs from a wildfire salvage harvest. (photo courtesy of the Georgia Forestry Commission)

Seeding skid trails protects soil after thinning operation and offers wildlife browse. (photo courtesy of the Georgia Forestry Commission)

Water bars on skid trails minimize soil erosion. (photo courtesy of the Georgia Forestry Commission)

Best Management Practices and Forest Health

• Research supports that silvicultural operations are minor contributors to nonpoint source pollution to State waters (< 3 percent) (U.S. Environmental Protection Agency 2005). Since 1981 when best management practices (BMP) began in Georgia, the percentage of acres in compliance has increased from 86 to 99.4 percent. The percentage of BMP implementation by silvicultural operations has increased from almost 65 percent to almost 90 percent.

• The southern pine beetle (SPB) continues to be Georgia's greatest threat to forest health causing periodic epidemic outbreaks mostly in the Piedmont and mountains. The average annual timber loss is about $7.4 million.

• Down woody materials data indicate that forest fuel loads for Georgia average 16 tons per acre, suggesting an equal or lower risk for forest fire than adjacent States.

• Statewide, tree crown conditions are within expected ranges and are not indicative of degraded forest health.

Temporary bridge using logs to protect water quality. (photo courtesy of the Georgia Forestry Commission)

Cypress pond. (photo courtesy of the Georgia Forestry Commission)

Forest Area

Trends in Forest Area

For the last 50 years, Georgia's forest land area has remained stable averaging 24.7 million acres. During the 2004 survey, almost 24.8 million acres, or 67 percent of the 37.1 million acres of land area, were forest land (fig. 1). Forest land area classified as timberland (capable of growing 20 cubic feet of wood per acre annually and available for commercial harvesting) occupied 24.2 million acres in 2004. Georgia contains the largest timberland area of all the States in the South, and timberland accounted for 65 percent of the total land area in Georgia. Parks, wilderness areas, historic sites, and other forest land where commercial timber harvesting is prohibited are known as reserved forest land. These areas account for the remaining 0.5 million acres or 2 percent of all forest land. Only 31,000 acres were classified as other forest land, which is not capable of growing 20 cubic feet of wood per acre annually because of adverse site conditions, such as dry rock outcrop areas, deep sands, or marsh coastal environments.

The State is divided into five survey units that typically follow physiographical regions (fig. 2). The Southeast and Southwest Survey Units coincide with the Coastal Plain region and the Central and North Central Survey Units encompass most of the Piedmont region. The North Survey Unit contains the upper Piedmont and the Mountain Province. Each unit has distinctive land features that allow for regional analysis of the forest resources.

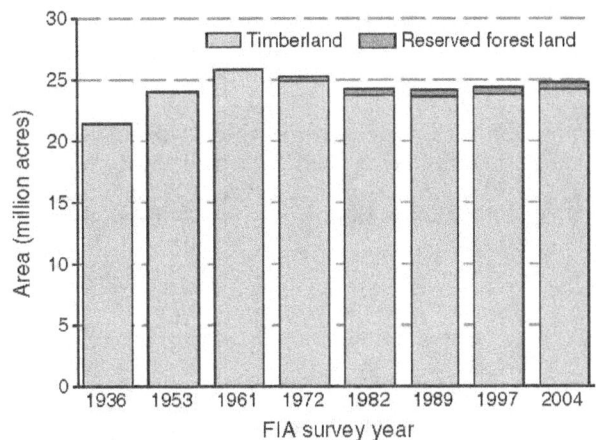

Figure 1—Timberland area by survey completion date, Georgia.

Figure 2—Forest survey units in Georgia.

The three southern survey units contain 74 percent of the timberland area and have added a net of 1.2 million acres of timberland since 1982 (Sheffield and Knight 1984). The North and North Central Survey Units have experienced a steady decline in timberland acres since 1972, although the North Survey Unit shows a stabilized timberland area since 1997 (Knight and McClure 1974). The net loss of timberland acres in these two northern units combined was almost 1.0 million acres since 1972.

These changes in land use have shifted the location of timberland throughout the State. Of greatest concern is the loss of timberland to urban development where deforestation occurs. Only in rare occurrences will developed land revert back to commercial forests. However, timberland and agricultural land have exchanged land use back and forth over time. Most recent incentives from government cost-share programs for afforestation combined with favorable timber markets during the 1980s and 1990s, have encouraged the reversion of agriculture land back to timberland,

especially in the three survey units in the southern portion of Georgia. Estimated agricultural land planted during this survey cycle was 748,000 acres or 29 percent of the 2.6 million acres planted between 1998 and 2004 (U.S. Department of Agriculture, unpublished data). This, in part, has led to the stability of timberland area over time and contributed to the increase of 450,000 acres in timberland since 1997. About 1.1 million acres reverted to timberland since 1997 with most of this gain in southeast and central Georgia (table 1).

Accessible timberland area declines with increase in population density (people per square mile). With an array of employment opportunities, a temperate climate, and a diverse landscape, Georgia offers residents and visitors diverse opportunities for quality of life. It is no wonder that Georgia had 16 of the fastest growing counties in the United States between 2000 and 2006 (U.S. Department of Commerce 2007). Fourteen counties were within a 50-mile radius of Atlanta and the remaining two were near Savannah.

Table 1—Changes in area of timberland by survey unit, Georgia, 1997 to 2004

| | Area of timberland in | | | | Changes | | | | | | |
| | | | | | Additions from | | | Diversions to | | | |
Survey unit	1997	2004	Net change	Total gain	Non-forest	Other forest land	Total loss	Other forest land	Agri-culture	Urban and other	Water
					thousand acres						
Southeast	7,244.3	7,667.3	423.0	583.9	583.9	—	160.9	—	53.4	92.7	14.8
Southwest	2,869.7	2,856.3	-13.4	67.4	67.4	—	80.8	7.7	46.3	18.1	8.7
Central	7,344.1	7,501.1	157.1	251.1	251.1	—	94.1	—	20.4	66.1	7.5
North Central	3,482.5	3,362.1	-120.4	104.4	104.4	—	224.9	—	40.2	177.0	7.7
North	2,855.6	2,859.8	4.2	84.4	84.4	—	80.2	—	19.9	57.6	2.7
State	23,796.1	24,246.5	450.4	1,091.3	1,091.3	—	640.8	7.7	180.2	411.5	41.4

Numbers in rows and columns may not sum to totals due to rounding.
— = no sample for the cell.

Timberland losses were estimated to be about 640,800 acres between 1997 and 2004. The estimated loss to development was 411,500 acres and 180,000 acres were converted to agriculture. As expected the greatest loss to development occurred in the North Central Survey Unit, which encompasses the Atlanta metropolitan area and the I-85 corridor from South Carolina to Alabama where population densities are greater (fig. 3).

Of the 411,500 acres of timberland converted to development in Georgia, 43 percent occurred in the North Central Survey Unit. The second greatest loss to development occurred in the Southeast Survey Unit where almost 23 percent was converted to development. However, the Southeast Survey Unit experienced the greatest gain in timberland which represented almost 54 percent of timberland additions resulting in a net increase of timberland area of almost 423,000 acres.

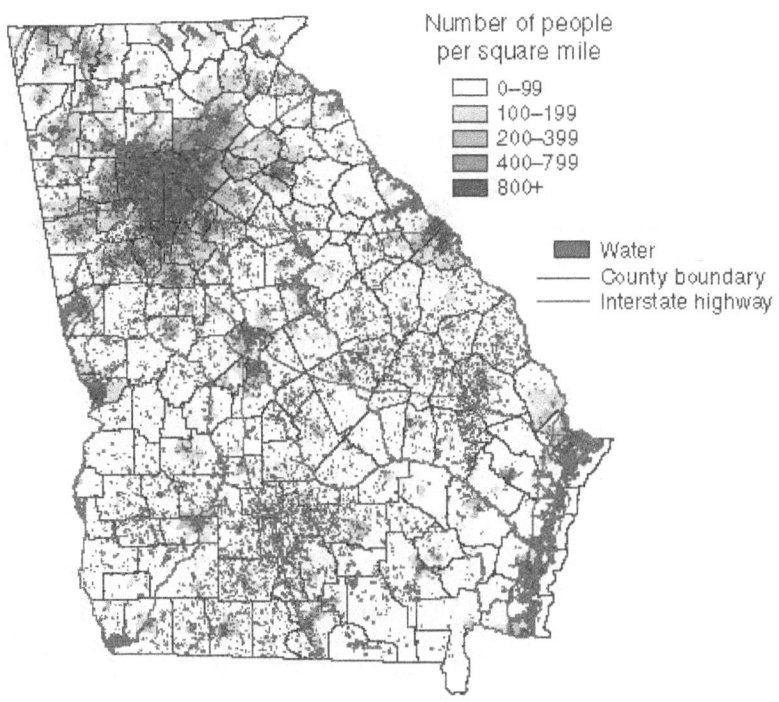

Number of people per square mile

☐ 0–99
☐ 100–199
☐ 200–399
☐ 400–799
■ 800+

■ Water
— County boundary
— Interstate highway

Figure 3—Population density Georgia, 2004.

Land-use change—development constantly carves away timberland. (photo courtesy of the Georgia Forestry Commission)

Grazing is one of many multiple uses on timberland. (photo courtesy of the Georgia Forestry Commission)

Evaluating the area of timberland in a survey unit converted to development divided by the total timberland in a survey unit offers a slightly different assessment. Again, the North Central Survey Unit experienced the largest loss of 177,000 acres of timberland which represented more than 5 percent of the timberland area in the unit. The North Survey Unit encountered a 2-percent loss of all timberland in the unit to development or about 57,600 acres. While the Southeast Survey Unit converted around 92,700 acres to development, it represented about 1.2 percent of timberland in the unit. The remaining Central and Southwest Survey Units converted < 1 percent of the timberland to development.

Review of the land use change by survey period offers an estimate of general land use trends (fig. 4). Total gain of timberland has edged out total loss which accounted for the stability of total timberland area over time. Review of timberland converted

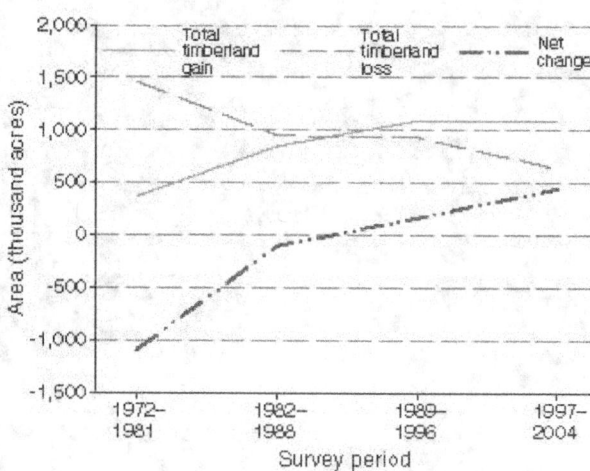

Figure 4—Land use change by survey period, Georgia.

to some form of development other than agriculture shows a relatively consistent acreage loss in each survey period which averaged about 432,000 acres for the four survey periods.

Increasing human population can be a double-edged sword—creating demand for forest products while changing the landscape from rural forestry and agricultural land use to urban development. The Atlanta metropolitan area and the I-85 corridor is a case-in-point.

Recent studies indicate that as population density increases to approximately 150 people per square mile, opportunities to practice forestry approach zero (Wear and others 1999). Another indicator of land use change from forestry is the increase of road network densities which fragment large area ownerships into parcels of small ownerships (Vickery and others 2009). Historically and as indicated in figure 3, land use conversion to development tends to expand in and around urban centers and along major trade routes.

Ownership

Forest Inventory and Analysis (FIA) classifies ownership into two general ownership categories: public lands and private lands. National forest lands, which is included in public timberlands, represented <3 percent of all timberland or 0.6 million acres (fig. 5). Public timberland also includes other public timberland which represents about 5 percent. Other public timberland includes other Federal lands (i.e., U.S. Fish and Wildlife, Department of Defense, Department of Energy, and others), State, county, and municipal lands.

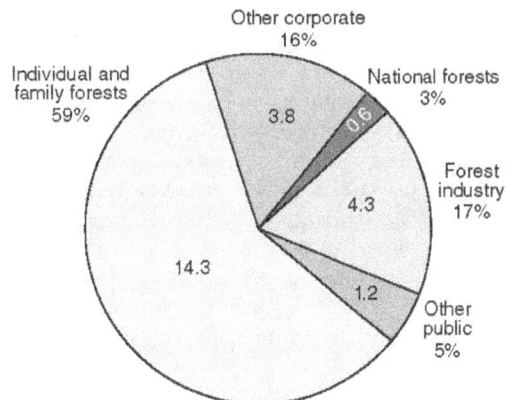

Total timberland = 24.2 million acres

Figure 5—Distribution of timberland ownership in Georgia, 2004.

All private ownerships hold 92 percent of the State's timberlands or 22.4 million acres. Private ownership is divided into forest industry lands (who also own a primary wood processing plant) and nonindustrial private forest (NIPF) ownership. In 2004, the forest industry owned 4.3 million acres or 17 percent of the timberland.

NIPF ownership is primarily divided into corporate and individual (or family) ownerships. The corporate ownership includes Timber Investment Management Organizations (TIMO), Real Estate Investment Trusts (REIT), Limited Liability Companies (LLC), and other incorporated ownerships. These landowners controlled 3.8 million acres or 16 percent of the timberland in Georgia.

The private individual and family ownerships have the most influence on timberland throughout the South. In Georgia, these NIPF owners control 14.3 million acres or more than 59 percent of the timberland.

Since 1972 the area of public timberland has increased 248,200 acres, while all private decreased almost 840,700 acres. Timberland ownership has always experienced movement from one group to another, but the majority occurs in the private ownership category. As an example, forest industry aggressively acquired timberland from the late 1940s through the 1970s as a basis for ensuring wood supply to their mills. With peak land holdings in the 1980s, they began to strategically consolidate tracts and sold outlying parcels to other forest industry or individuals. Some companies with landholdings located near growing suburban areas formed real estate subsidiaries to market these lands for commercial and residential development. Nonindustrial owners also took advantage of suburban growth and developed or sold their timberlands to other land uses.

Throughout the 1990s and into the turn of the century, market pressures, tax policy, industry consolidation, and an abundant wood supply were catalysts for a new wave of ownership change. The vertically integrated forest industry made the decision to divest landholdings. Large tracts of timberland shifted from direct control by large industry to corporate ownerships such as TIMOs or REITs, usually with some long-term wood supply agreement attached. Some timberland was sold to small forest industries and individuals. From 1982 to 2004, industry ownership decreased by more than 1.6 million acres and corporate ownership increased almost 2 million acres. Private individual and family ownership decreased slightly during this period (fig. 6). Some of the decrease was a result of movement to the corporate category as more family ownerships sought less personal liability by incorporating their timberland into an LLC.

Forest Types

Containing five physiographic provinces, Georgia offers a diverse landscape from the Appalachian Plateau and Blue Ridge Mountains through the Piedmont to the Atlantic Coastal Plain. With over 150 tree species found on FIA plots in Georgia, there are numerous softwood and hardwood forest cover types that occupy forest land.

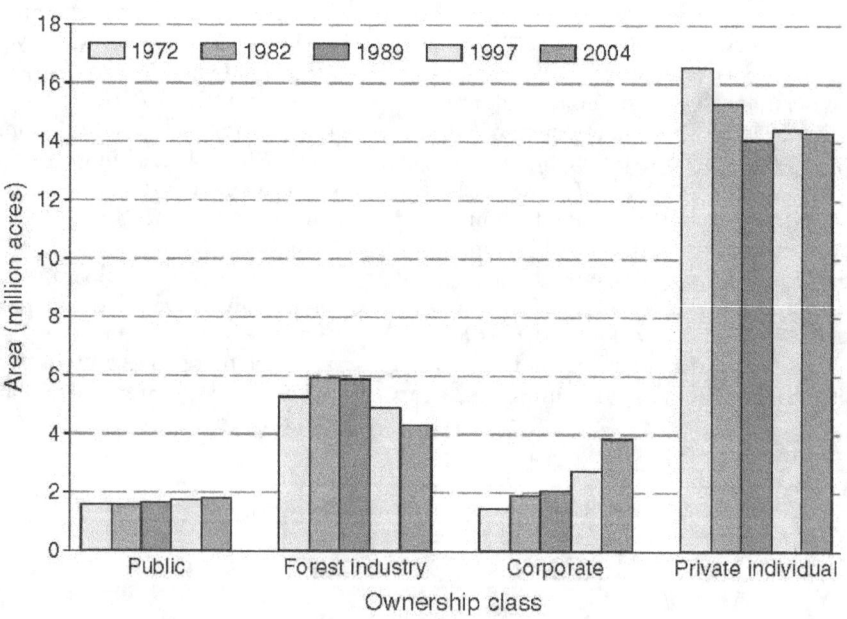

Figure 6—Area of timberland in Georgia by ownership class and survey completion date.

Loblolly pine forest type represents 28 percent of all timberland. (photo courtesy of the Georgia Forestry Commission)

FIA identifies the two major forest types as softwood and hardwood. Softwood area accounts for almost 10.8 million acres or 45 percent of timberland, and hardwood represents almost 55 percent with 13.2 million acres. The major forest types are grouped to simplify the many possibilities of forest-type description. The forest-type groups for Georgia include:

Softwood	Hardwood
White pine	Oak-pine
Longleaf-slash	Oak-hickory
Loblolly-shortleaf	Oak-gum-cypress
Eastern redcedar	Elm-ash-cottonwood
	Tropical-exotic hardwood

Loblolly-shortleaf was the predominate forest-type group with 7.3 million acres in 2004 which represented 31 percent of the timberland in Georgia. The loblolly-shortleaf area increased 144,000 acres or 2 percent since 1997. Within this group is the loblolly forest type which is the predominate forest type in Georgia with 6.8 million acres representing 28 percent of all timberland. Because of its successful regeneration, high productivity, and valuable wood products loblolly pine continues to be the favored species in Georgia and gained 283,000 acres (4 percent). Loblolly pine also accounted for the largest acreage in plantations with 4.1 million acres or 17 percent of the timberland area. This was an increase of 214,000 acres or 5 percent of the total planted loblolly area. Since 1997, natural loblolly stands increased by 69,000 acres.

Oak-hickory forest-type group represents 27 percent of all timberland. (photo by Melissa Carlson)

Shortleaf and Virginia pine types continued to experience a decline in area as these species are often supplanted by loblolly. In 2004, there were 192,000 and 198,000 acres, respectively. Shortleaf area declined 33 percent losing 95,000 acres since 1997, while Virginia pine lost 29,000 acres representing a 13-percent loss of area.

Longleaf-slash was the third largest forest-type group in Georgia with almost 3.5 million acres or just over 14 percent of the timberland area. This forest-type group experienced a modest increase of 2 percent or 52,000 acres from 1997 to 2004.

Restoration efforts have achieved a 23-percent increase in the longleaf pine forest type since 1997. Longleaf pine plantations averaged more than 17,000 acres a year during this survey and contributed to the total of 464,000 acres in 2004, an increase of 87,000 acres. Longleaf pine has experienced a long-term decline and this marks the first increase of area in decades.

Slash pine forest-type area stabilized after the 15-percent decline in area that was reported in 1997 (Thompson and Thompson 2002). It experienced a 1-percent decrease in area and occupied almost 3.0 million acres or 12 percent of the timberland. Together, slash and loblolly forest types contribute 91 percent of all softwood forest types and more than 40 percent of all timberland in Georgia.

Despite what seems to be favoritism toward southern yellow pine, Georgia timberland area contains more hardwood area. Oak-pine is included in the hardwood forest types causing total hardwood area to exceed softwood area by 2.4 million acres.

The oak-pine forest-type group contains both pine and hardwood species. For a forest type to be considered oak-pine, the pine species stocking must be between 25 to 50 percent of all live trees. The oak-pine forest-type group lost slightly more area (575,000 acres) during this survey period than it gained in the 1997 survey and now comprises 12 percent of the timberland. Changes in stocking, due to stand dynamics and harvesting treatments, can shift from softwood forest types to upland hardwood forest types. For example, nearly 600,000 acres showed evidence of past pine planting or seeding that now has a large hardwood component.

In terms of area, the oak-hickory type group is second only to the loblolly-shortleaf type group. This upland hardwood group increased 1.1 million acres or 21 percent since the 1997 survey. Total area in 2004 was 6.6 million acres marking an all-time high. A large portion of this gain may be attributed to the reduction of the oak-pine forest-type group shifting into oak-hickory through the removal of pine by harvesting or tree mortality from insects and disease. On average, pine species have a shorter life cycle than the climatic forest type of oak-hickory.

Lowland or bottomland hardwoods represent those hardwood types located in wet flatwood sites, along streams and rivers, or in swamps. They are concentrated in the Coastal Plain area of the Southeast and Southwest Survey Units, but can occur throughout most of Georgia. There are two diverse forest-type groups: oak-gum-cypress and elm-ash-cottonwood. Together these timber stands make up 15 percent of Georgia's timberland, consisting

of 3.6 million acres. Combined, these two hardwood forest-type groups declined almost 159,000 acres or 4 percent since 1997. However, due to changes in forest-type algorithms for some lowland forest types, it is difficult to assess individual change within these two forest-type groups for this survey period.

Forest land currently stocked with <10 percent of live trees is considered nonstocked. These areas are usually in transition to a stocked stand due to some type of harvesting, disturbance, or reversion of old fields to forest land.

Figure 7 shows the current area in each of the forest-type groups just described. There are other forest types not shown on the chart that include white pine, eastern redcedar, tropical hardwood, and exotic hardwood. Combined, these forest types represent about 0.3 percent of the timberland area.

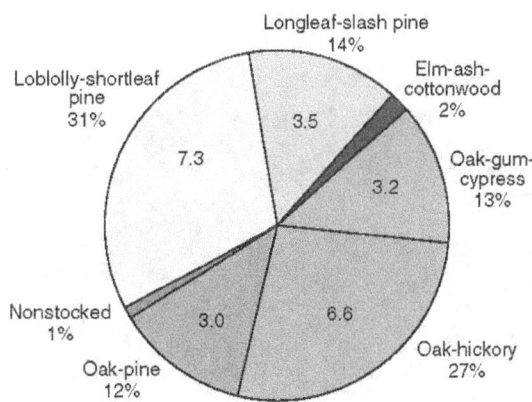

Total timberland = 24.2 million acres

Figure 7—Distribution of forest-type groups on timberland, Georgia, 2004.

Forest Management Types

Forest-type groups are sometimes arranged as forest management types. These six categories broadly demonstrate the influence of forest management on the landscape and how these areas have changed. Forest management types include:

Planted pine   Natural pine
Oak-pine   Upland hardwood
Lowland hardwood   Nonstocked

The most prominent change occurred in the pine cover type. The 1972 survey reported 12.3 million acres in pine cover types (Knight and McClure 1974). At that time, natural pine dominated the softwood type occupying 9.4 million acres or 76 percent of the softwood area and planted pine totaled 2.8 million acres. However, tree planting of southern yellow pine (predominately loblolly) has had a tremendous impact on the forest landscape in Georgia. From 1972 to 2004, Georgia planted more than 10 million acres (U.S. Department of Agriculture, unpublished data) (fig. 8). At the end of the Federal Soil Bank Program that provided incentives for tree planting on nonindustrial land, forest industry led the way from the early 1960s through the 1970s, planting almost 1.5 million acres. Fueled by a new wave of government cost-share incentives, such as the Conservation Reserve Program and promising timber markets, nonindustrial forest landowners comprised of individuals, families, farmers, and others planted 5.1 million acres from 1980 to 2004 compared to industry's 3.9 million acres. By 2004, the planted pine management type area accounted for almost 6.5 million acres or 60 percent of the 10.8 million acres of softwood area even though total pine cover had declined 1.5 million acres since 1972.

Since 1997, the increase in planted pine area moderated to some extent, but still added 410,000 acres representing a 7-percent increase (fig. 9). Pine plantation area increased in all units except the North Central Survey Unit where planted area

Planted longleaf pine management has helped to restore the longleaf pine in Georgia. (SRS photo)

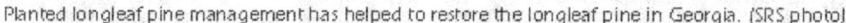

decreased 22,000 acres since 1997, down to 380,000 acres. The greatest increase occurred in the Southeast Survey Unit where 251,000 acres (9 percent) were added since 1997, bringing the total to 3.0 million acres of pine plantations. The Central Survey Unit added almost 84,000 acres of planted pine stands for a total of 2.0 million acres while the Southwest Survey Unit added almost 73,000 acres for a total of 787,000 acres. Combined, these three units have 5.9 million acres of pine plantations or 90 percent of the planted pine area in Georgia.

From 1972 to 2004, natural pine area declined 5.1 million acres leaving a residual of 4.3 million acres. The decline since 1997 amounted to a loss of 300,000 acres or almost 7 percent. The improvements in site preparation and tree planting survival, reforestation cost-share and tax incentives, along with genetically improved seedlings offer a cost-effective alternative forest management option and have contributed to the conversion of many natural stands to planted stands after harvesting.

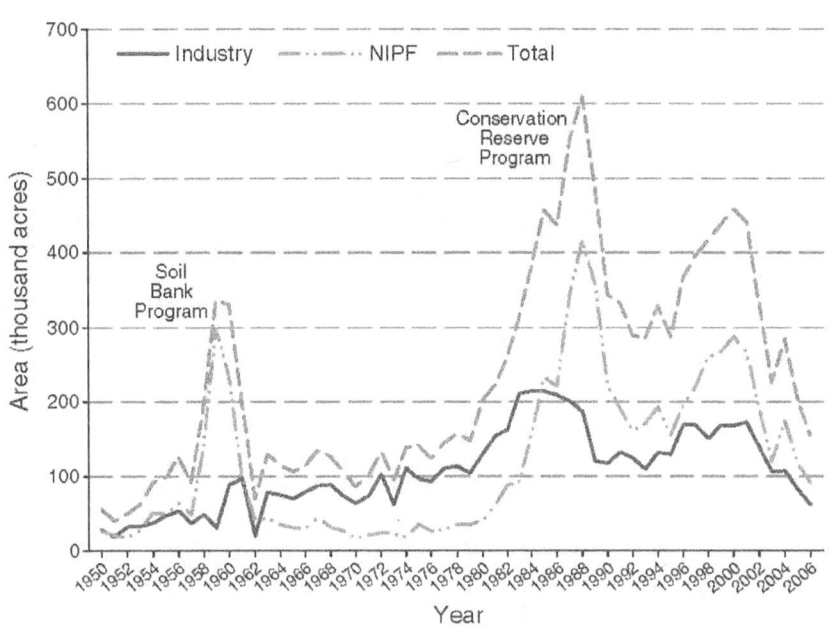

Figure 8—Tree planting area in Georgia from 1950–2006; (NIPF = nonindustrial private forest) total includes State and local government, national forest, and other forest land.

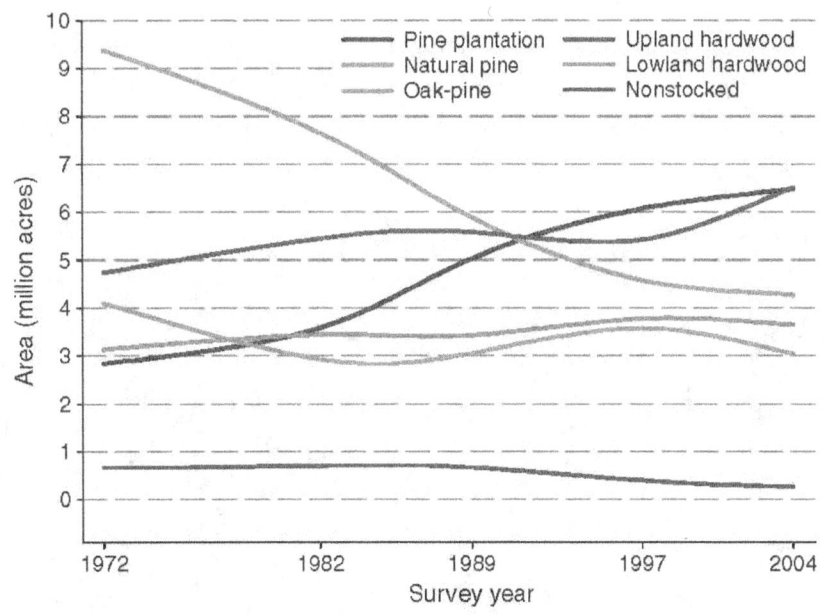

Figure 9—Area of timberland in Georgia by forest-management type and survey completion date.

As discussed above, the species mix in oak-pine stands moves in and out of upland hardwood and can be converted to planted pine stands after harvesting. At 4.1 million acres in 1972, the area oscillated slightly over time and had declined to 3.0 million acres by 2004. Upland hardwood, composed primarily of oak-hickory forest types has remained fairly stable over time and may include portions of exotic-tropical hardwood types. However, the upland hardwood type experienced a 20-percent gain of 1.1 million acres since 1997 to its highest level.

Lowland hardwood has shown an increase of more than 495,500 acres in area since 1972, although there was a slight decline since the 1997 survey of almost 145,600 acres. Gains and losses of this management type occur mostly along the edge transition zone (ecotones) to upland hardwood and agricultural lands. Most forest operations are limited to seasonal activity during dry conditions and stands regenerate naturally.

Forests have always experienced change through natural dynamics of stand succession, fire, and catastrophic events, or have been induced by human utilization and land use change. The remarkable feature of forest disturbance and management is the resilience of the forest resources to restore the landscape to a diverse and productive forest ecosystem.

Cypress stand in lowland hardwood management type. (SRS photo)

Inventory Volume

The change in inventory volume of timberland is primarily influenced by change in timberland area, diameter distribution, trees per acre, and the application of timberland management methods. Since 1953, all live-tree volume has increased 16.0 billion cubic feet or 78 percent (Knight and McClure 1974). The greatest change occurred from 1961 to 1982 increasing 52 percent, then volume remained relatively stable until 2004 when volume experienced an upturn of almost 3.0 billion cubic feet, a 9-percent increase (fig. 10).

Softwood Inventory

The 2004 total softwood volume stands at 17.7 billion cubic feet, surpassing the 1982 peak by almost 1.0 billion cubic feet. The boost in total volume (softwood and hardwood) since the 1997 survey is primarily attributed to softwood volume which increased 2.4 billion cubic feet or almost 16 percent (fig. 10). Most of the softwood volume increase from 1997 to 2004 can be attributed to tree planting in the 1980s and 1990s. Planted softwood volume increased 2.1 billion cubic feet for a total of 6.7 billion cubic feet, or 40 percent of the total softwood volume.

Softwood volume had its greatest surge of 38 percent in the 11-year period from 1961 to 1972 adding 4.3 billion cubic feet. Another 1.0 billion cubic feet in volume was added by 1982, then a decline occurred over the next two surveys losing more than 1.4 billion cubic feet by 1997.

With almost 10.0 billion cubic feet, loblolly pine dominated slash pine by more than 2.4 to 1. Loblolly volume increased by 2.0 million cubic feet or almost 24 percent since 1997 (fig. 11).

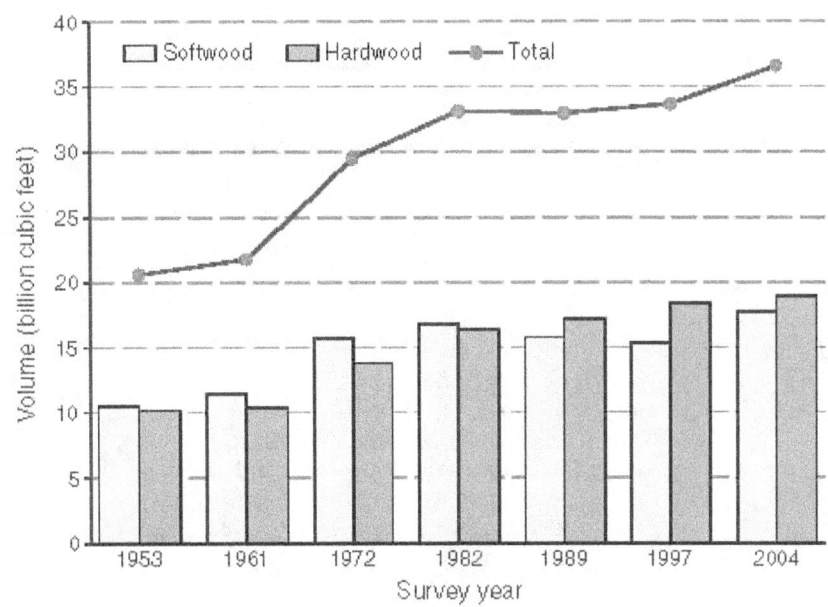

Figure 10—Volume of all live trees on timberland by species group and survey completion date, Georgia.

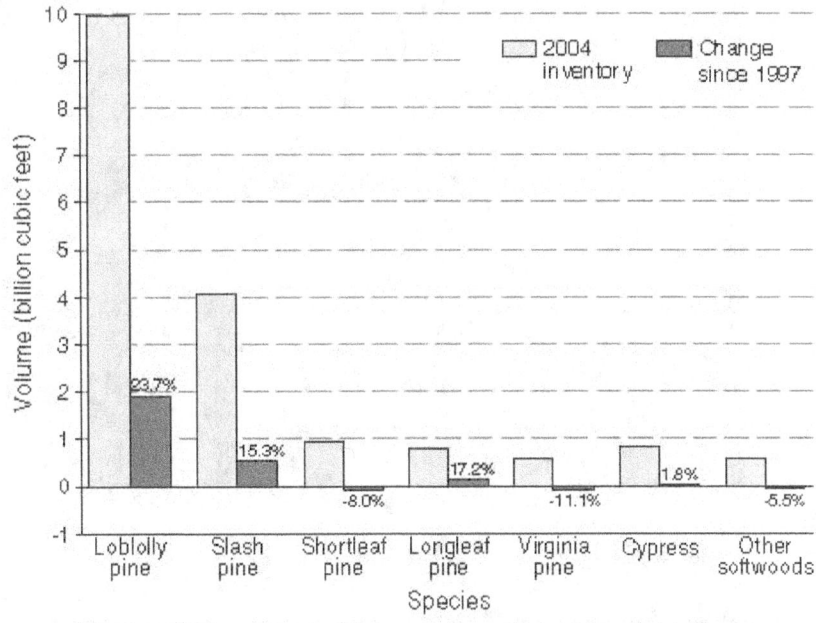

Figure 11—Volume of softwood live trees in Georgia by species, 2004, and volume change since 1997.

In 2004, loblolly accounted for 56 percent of the softwood inventory volume. Slash pine is the next dominant species and accounted for 23 percent of all softwood volume with over 4 billion cubic feet. Combined, loblolly and slash pine accounted for 79 percent of the softwood volume. In conjunction with the increase in area, longleaf pine also marked a 17-percent volume increase to 0.8 billion cubic feet. The remaining dominant pine species, shortleaf and Virginia pine, declined in volume 8 and 11 percent, respectively.

Diameter class distribution is another way to assess change of volume and perhaps offers insight for future volume. During the last four survey periods (i.e., 1982, 1989, 1997, and 2004), softwood volumes in the

14- to 20-inch diameter classes have tracked closely, indicating that incremental growth is closely replacing loss in those diameter classes (fig. 12). The combined volume of the large diameters of 22 inches and greater has shown a steady increase, and have more than doubled since 1982. Most of the large diameter volume is in natural pine stands.

Volume in the 10- to 12-inch diameter classes experienced an unusual decline from 1982 to 1997. For example, the 10-inch diameter class decreased 0.59 billion cubic feet, or 19 percent, and the 12-inch diameter class decreased 0.47 billion cubic feet, or 17 percent. Throughout the South, harvesting levels during the early to mid-1990s reached an all-time high as harvesting from Federal lands declined in

Managed stands increase volume per acre. (SRS photo)

the West. Average annual removals increased for all diameter classes from 1989 to 1997, with the greatest volume removed in the 8- to 12-inch diameter classes (Thompson and Thompson 2002).

Removals, discussed in greater detail later in this bulletin, continued to increase for the 6-, 8-, and 10-inch diameter classes for the period between 1997 and 2004. However, it is evident that the volume from the increased area of planted pine and some natural pine stands began to appear in the smaller diameter classes. Planted pine (loblolly, slash, and longleaf) volume for the 6-, 8-, 10-, and 12-inch diameter classes increased 21, 33, 25, and 11 percent, respectively. Natural pine stands had little influence on volume in the 6- and 8-inch diameter classes. Natural pine volume declined in the 10-inch class, while the 12-inch class experienced no change.

Linking the volume by diameter classes with age-class volumes offers insight into the impact of planted pine stands. The increase in merchantable volume made a dramatic appearance beginning in the 11- to 15-year age class, totaling 1.2 billion cubic feet in 2004 (fig. 13). Volume increased 31 percent since 1997 with 90 percent of the volume in the 6- and 8-inch diameter classes (table 2).

The 16- to 20-year age class experienced a remarkable increase of almost 99 percent since 1997 totaling 2.2 billion cubic feet in 2004 (fig. 13). Most of the volume was distributed across the 6-, 8-, and 10-inch diameter classes, with 45 percent in the 8-inch class (table 2).

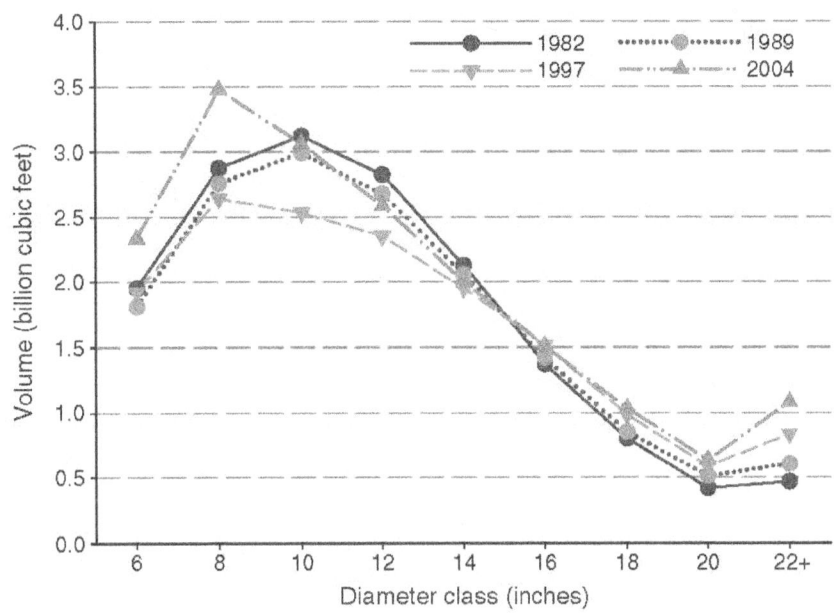

Figure 12—Merchantable volume of softwood live trees in Georgia by diameter class and survey completion date.

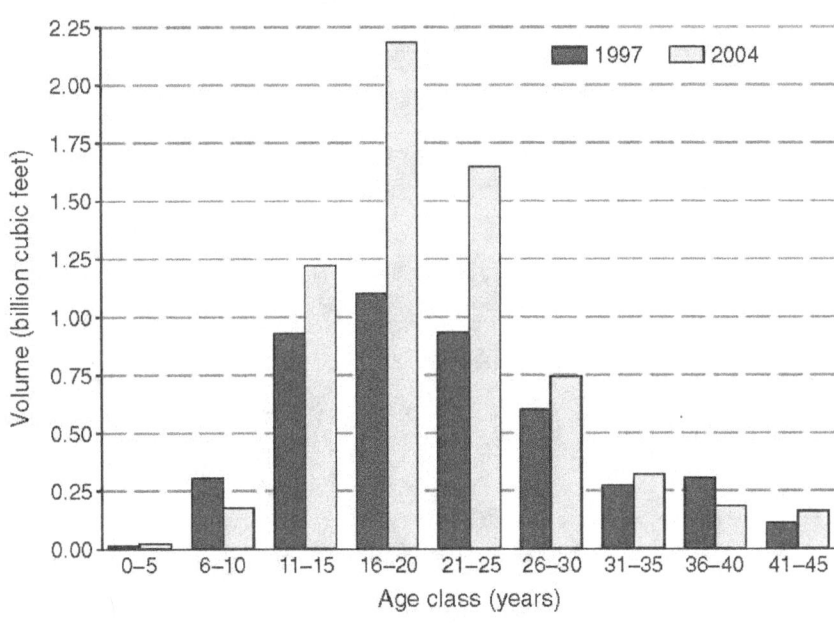

Figure 13—Volume of planted pine in Georgia by age class for survey periods 1997 and 2004.

Table 2—Percent of volume in diameter classes by age class for planted pine, Georgia, 2004

Age class years	Diameter class (*inches at breast height*)					
	5.0–6.9	7.0–8.9	9.0–10.9	11.0–12.9	13.0–14.9	15.0–16.9
	percent					
11–15	51	39	8	1	0	0
16–20	26	45	23	5	1	0
21–25	14	35	31	15	4	1
26–30	7	20	33	24	8	4
31–35	5	22	32	26	7	6

The second largest increase in volume for planted pine stands occurred in the 21- to 25-year age class, with a 76-percent increase since 1997. Volume totaled more than 1.6 billion cubic feet and was distributed across four diameter classes with some volume also appearing in the 14- to 16-inch classes. Figure 13 shows volume dropped noticeably in the 26- to 30-year age class to 0.74 billion cubic feet, but increased 24 percent since 1997. Volume continued to spread out over

a broader range of diameter classes, as would be expected.

Also of interest is the shift in softwood live-tree volume across age classes. The 1989, 1997, and 2004 data show comparable volumes in the age classes for 46 years and greater (fig. 14). The shift occurred from the 26- to 45-year age classes for the 1989 survey, which declined 40 percent or almost 3.0 billion cubic feet by 2004 to the 11- to 30-year age classes, which gained 3.5 billion cubic feet. The volume of these age classes increased 84 percent since 1989 and 74 percent of this volume was comprised of pine plantations (Sheffield and Johnson 1993).

It is important to note that age class estimation in the field can be somewhat subjective in mixed age stands, but should offer a reasonable estimation in planted pine stands. The apparent peak in volume for the 16-20 and 21-25 age classes is most likely attributed to an increase in the number of plots that fall in planted pine

Figure 14—Distribution of softwood live-tree volume in Georgia by age class for the 1989, 1997, and 2004 surveys.

Planted pine on agriculture land is known as aforestation. (photo courtesy of the Georgia Forestry Commission)

stands in these age classes for this survey period (2004) and, thus, the increase in area and volume. Georgia and other States across the South experienced a change in the plot list to establish one plot per hex that could confound comparisons and trend analysis during the methodology transition from periodic to annual inventory. Despite these changes, it is clear that there has been a substantial increase in softwood volume in pine plantations in Georgia. Refer to the Methods section for more information.

What influence might the increased tree planting have on future pine volume? Figure 12 demonstrates that the 2004 volume of the 6- and 8-inch diameter classes exceeded any previous survey volume and the 10-inch class recovered very close to the 1982 peak volume. If these stands are effectively managed until age 30 and harvest levels are maintained close to current levels, the 10-, 12-, and 14-inch

diameter classes are expected to exceed the 1982 volume level during the next 10 years and provide 70 percent of the saw-log/veneer wood supply. In addition, saw log and veneer logs would potentially be available from natural pine stands which contained more than three times the saw-log volume on pine plantations in 2004. The volume in the 6- and 8-inch diameter classes will likely decline in 10 years as tree planting area has declined in recent years (fig. 8).

As with any estimates of future trends, it is difficult to predict unexpected events. These estimates do not account for catastrophic events, such as hurricanes, fires, or epidemic insect outbreaks. Significant shifts in land use and influence of regional and global market fluctuations also could impact the production from pine plantations in Georgia.

Hardwood volume has been increasing over the last 50 years in Georgia. (photo courtesy of the Georgia Forestry Commission)

Hardwood Inventory

Hardwood live-tree volume has increased in every survey since 1953. The greatest increase occurred in 1972 when volume jumped 3.4 billion cubic feet or 33 percent (fig. 10). During the next 10 years, hardwood continued to increase another 2.6 billion cubic feet to a total volume of 16.4 billion cubic feet. By 1989, hardwood volume exceeded softwood volume, and experienced a moderate 3-percent increase since 1997 to a peak of 18.9 billion cubic feet.

While there are 131 species of hardwoods in the FIA database for Georgia, the volume is best represented by the 9 dominant hardwood species groups:

Select white oaks	Other red oaks
Sweetgum	Select red oaks
Hickory	Tupelo-blackgum
Other white oaks	Soft maple
Yellow-poplar	

Unlike the softwood species group, none of the hardwood species groups dominated the landscape. Each group usually contained a large component of various hardwood species and often included a mix of softwood species.

The other red oaks species group had the largest volume totaling nearly 4.4 billion cubic feet, or 23 percent of the total hardwood volume (fig. 15). Other red oak volume increased almost 4 percent since 1997. The next three leading species groups were sweetgum (2.4 billion cubic feet), tupelo-blackgum (2.1 billion cubic feet), and yellow-poplar (2.2 billion cubic feet), representing 13, 11, and 12 percent of the hardwood volume, respectively. Of these three species groups, only the yellow-poplar group experienced an increase in volume (9 percent). Select white oaks and other white oaks increased 8 percent (1.6 billion cubic feet) and 5 percent (1.4 billion cubic feet), respectively. Since 1997, three species groups declined in volume, with the largest loss occurring in select red oaks (19 percent).

During the period 1982 to 2004, volume in most diameter classes remained relatively stable or increased (fig. 16). From 1997 to 2004, volume in all diameter classes increased except for the 12-inch class, which declined 3 percent and remains at or above historical levels. Since 1982, the greatest increase occurred in the 22-inch and greater classes with an 86-percent increase or almost 1.3 billion cubic feet.

Hardwood volume for 2004 has continued to increase in spite of increased harvest levels. Average annual removals increased for hardwoods in the 6-inch diameter class and the 12- through 16-inch diameter classes, which will be discussed later. For comparison, the timber product output (TPO) data showed an increase in hardwood pulpwood and composite mill

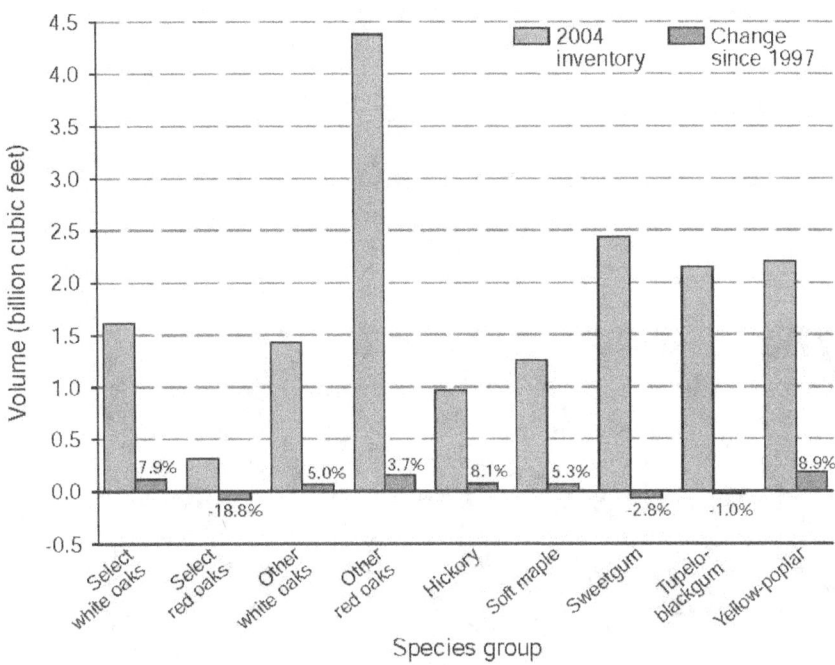

Figure 15—Volume of hardwood live trees in Georgia by species, 2004, and volume change since 1997.

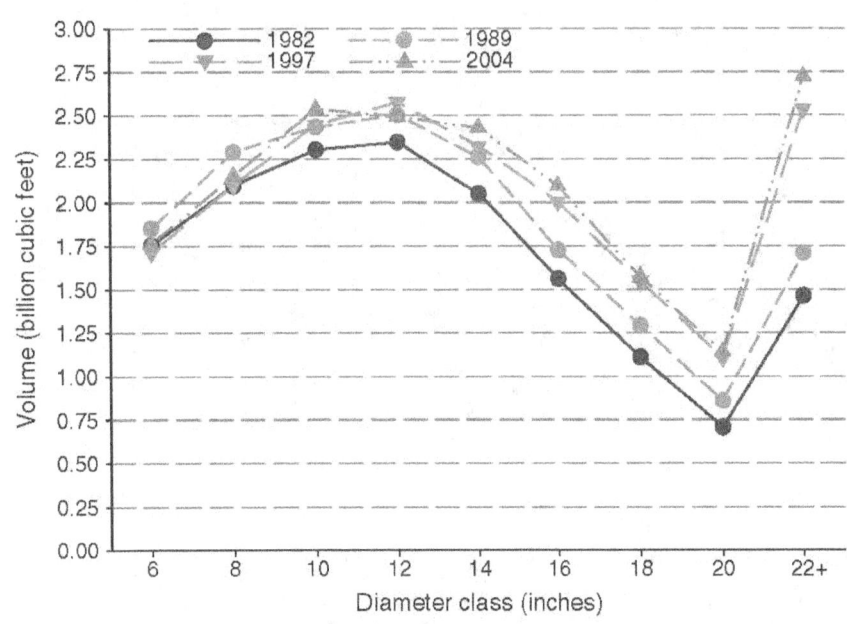

Figure 16—Volume of hardwood live trees by diameter class and survey completion date, Georgia, 2004.

consumption from 1992 to 2001. Compared to a base volume pulpwood production of almost 72 million cubic feet in 1983, the average production for TPO surveys 1997 to 2004 increased by 130 percent to 165 million cubic feet (Tansey and Steppleton 1991). Even with this increased roundwood production of hardwood, the volume remained relatively stable for the last two survey periods.

Hardwood live-tree volume by 5-year age classes appeared to be relatively stable. Two slight shifts have occurred since the 1989 survey. Combined volume in the younger age classes (6 to 25) show a notable 54-percent increase in volume, or 0.73 billion cubic feet. This is mostly attributed to the increase in area for these age classes, and represents a larger area for potential future growth into larger diameter classes. In 1989, the peak in hardwood volume ranged from 36- to 60-year age classes. This peak shifted to the older age classes (46 to 70) by 2004.

Volume by survey unit—With softwood volume up 16 percent and hardwood volume up 3 percent, each survey unit reflects where some of this change occurred (fig. 17). For the most part, softwood volume experienced a steady decline in the North and North Central Survey Units since 1989 dropping 12 and 6 percent, respectively. Some of this decline can be attributed to epidemic outbreaks of the SPB, and loss of acres to development. The Central, Southwest, and Southeast Survey Units experienced a slight decline in softwood volume between 1982 and 1997; however, all three rebounded to record high volumes by 2004. The Southeast Survey Unit experienced the largest increase since 1997 adding almost 1.2 billion cubic feet (24 percent). The Central and Southwest Survey Units gained 20 and 15 percent in softwood volume, respectively, and added 0.9 and 0.3 billion cubic feet. Combined, the three southern units contributed an additional 2.4 billion cubic feet of softwood volume since 1997, accounting for 98 percent of the net increase in softwood inventory volume in Georgia for 2004.

Since 1982, the increase in hardwood live-tree volume primarily occurred in the North and North Central Survey Units of Georgia.

Lowland hardwood stands offer diverse habitat. (photo by Bill Lea)

The North Central Survey Unit gained 1.3 billion cubic feet and increased 50 percent, but only added 1 percent since 1997. The North Survey Unit experienced a more consistent gain adding almost 1.2 billion cubic feet or a 43-percent increase since 1982. Since 1997, it increased 0.26 billion cubic feet, or 7 percent.

Since 1982, the Southeast Survey Unit added 6 percent or 0.24 billion cubic to the hardwood inventory volume, and the Central Survey Unit added 0.62 billion cubic feet or 13 percent. The Southwest Survey Unit hardwood inventory increased from 1982 to 1997, but experienced a decline of 4 percent since 1997.

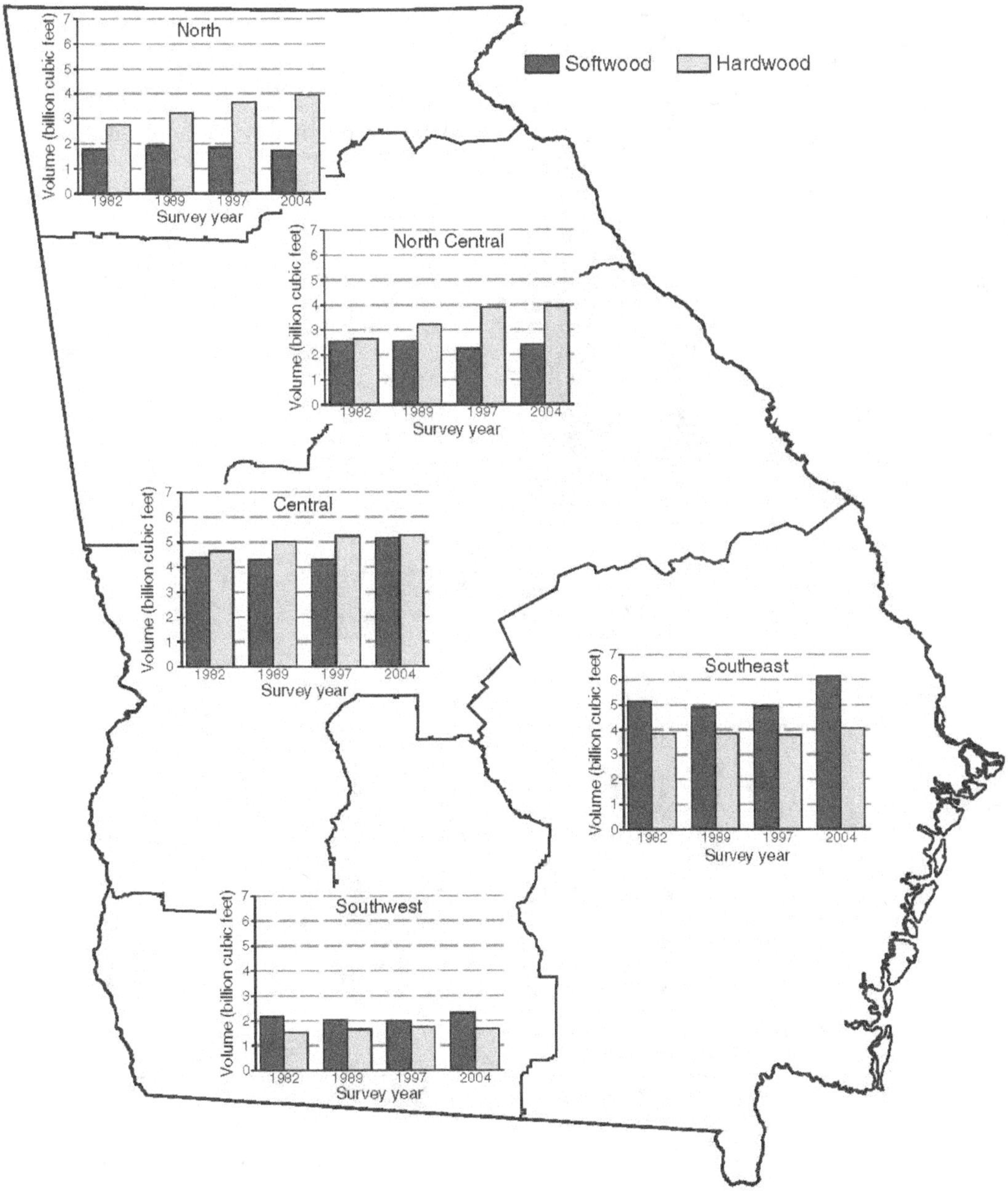

Figure 17—Volume of softwood and hardwood live trees on timberland in Georgia by survey unit and survey completion year.

Components of Change

Net growth, removals, and mortality (GRM) comprise the components of change in the forest inventory. GRM estimates are based on plots that were forested in the 2004 survey cycle or the previous survey cycle (1997). Estimates of each component are expressed as the average annual value between inventories. Net growth is the total (or gross) growth minus mortality. Net growth and removals reflect the internal dynamics (natural and human induced) of the forest resource and help evaluate how and why the forest inventory volume is increasing or decreasing.

Figure 18 shows the total average annual components of change of live-tree volume for three FIA surveys in Georgia. From a forest resource standpoint, the general trend shows that the forest inventory has increased from 1982 to 2004. In spite of increased removals, total volume was at an all-time high in 2004 (fig. 10).

When assessing the impact of net growth and removals, total volume must be included. Figure 19 places average annual net growth and removals on the same scale with total live-tree volume for the survey period. Net change (net growth minus removals) equals 0.4 billion cubic feet, an amount Georgia added annually (about 1 percent) to the total inventory between

Well managed mature pine stand. (photo courtesy of the Georgia Forestry Commission)

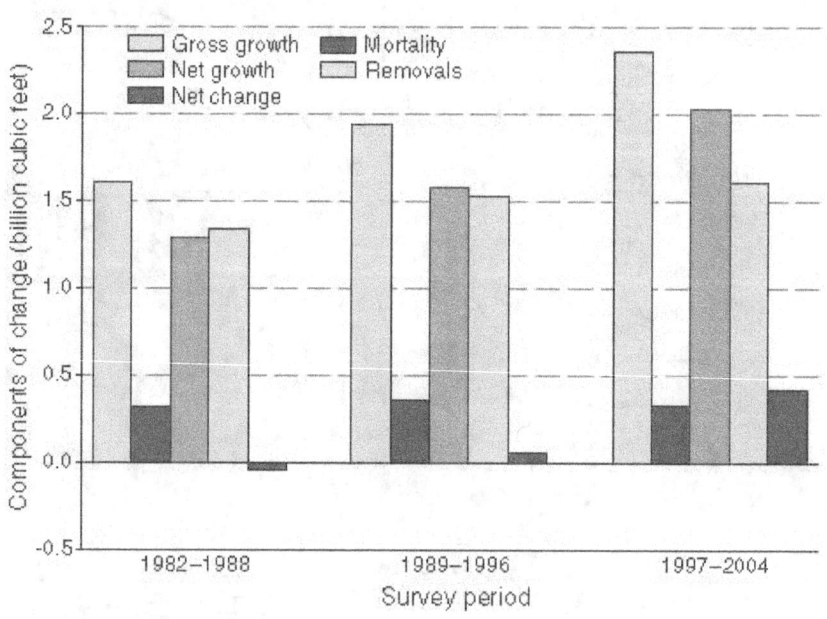

Figure 18—Average annual components of change for live trees in Georgia by survey period.

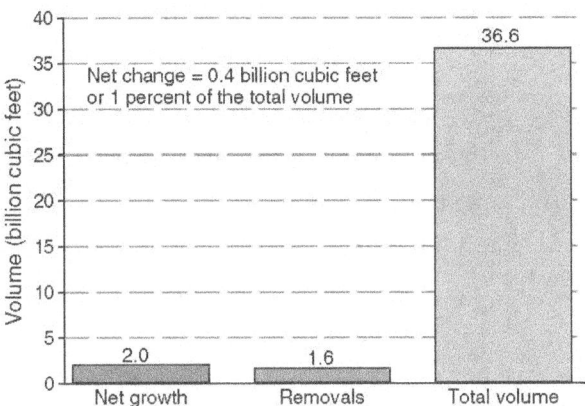

Figure 19—Average annual net growth and removals for live trees compared to total inventory volume in Georgia, 2004.

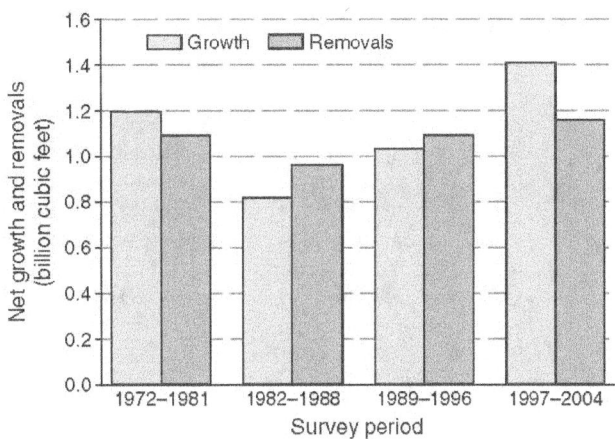

Figure 20—Average annual net growth and removals for softwood live trees in Georgia by survey period.

1997 and 2004. Although this annual increase in volume is substantial, the impact to total inventory volume is relatively small.

Softwood Average Annual Net Growth, Removals, and Mortality

Softwood average annual net growth represented 69 percent of the total growth in Georgia for 2004. From 1997 to 2004, an average of about 1.41 billion cubic feet of softwood live-tree volume was grown in the State each year. That was an increase of 36 percent from the last survey and continues the increase in growth since its last decline 22 years ago. Softwood average annual removals of live-tree volume have tracked a similar upward trend and exceeded growth until the 2004 survey cycle (fig. 20). The average annual removals totaled 1.16 billion cubic feet during the 1997 to 2004 survey period, an increase of 6 percent over the previous survey.

For this survey period, softwood net growth increased in all the major ownership classes except on national forest land where net growth declined 30 percent. The majority of the growth occurred on NIPF land

marking a 47-percent increase adding almost 304 million cubic feet annually. Net growth on forest industry lands increased 20 percent, while it increased 25 percent in the category of other public lands. Average annual removals increased 30 percent on forest industry timberland, while NIPF removals declined 1 percent. It is noteworthy that national forest land experienced a historic decrease in removals from 10.2 to 1.5 billion cubic feet and was the only ownership that also experienced a significant decline in softwood net growth.

Removals by diameter class indicate where much of the timber harvesting operations have occurred. Almost 70 percent of the softwood removals occurred in the 8- through 14-inch diameter classes combined, with each removing 147 to 250 million cubic feet annually. However, almost all of the increase in removals since 1997 occurred in the smaller diameter classes of 6 through 10 inches. Combined, the removals in these diameter classes increased 16 percent. Except for the 20-inch diameter class, the remaining classes experienced a decline in removals since 1997.

Growth per acre offers a comparison of growth rates without the confounding affect of land area changes (Thompson and Thompson 2002). During the 1997 survey, net growth averaged 44 cubic feet per acre per year, up from 33 cubic feet per acre per year in the 1989 survey. For 2004, the average net growth jumped to 59 cubic feet per acre per year. This is an indication that softwood productivity has increased significantly in the last 15 years, primarily from pine plantation productivity. The most dramatic increase occurred on forest industry land where the net annual growth average volume per acre increased from 57 to 81 cubic feet per acre per year. NIPF also marked a notable increase from 40 to 55 cubic feet per acre per year (fig. 21).

The average growth per acre per year was also estimated for all planted softwood stands on all ownerships in Georgia for 2004. This placed the average productivity of plantations at almost 138 cubic feet per acre per year or about 1.9 cords per acre per year which represents a 26-percent increase since 1997.

The relationship between net growth and removals from 1997 to 2004 shows that Georgia was growing 21 percent more softwood volume each year than was being removed through timber harvesting and changes in land use (fig. 22). This was a significant turnaround from the 1980s when softwood removals exceeded net growth by 18 percent. Since 1982, there was a slight decline in land area for softwood forest types and an increase in pine plantations of 2.9 million acres. It appears that increased net growth over removals can be attributed to increased production through effective management of timberland.

Softwood average annual mortality for Georgia declined 5 percent since 1997. The Southeast Survey Unit encountered a significant increase in average annual mortality of 6.5 million cubic feet, or 26 percent; and the North Survey Unit experienced a slight increase of 2 percent. The remaining three units posted a decrease in mortality ranging from 11 to 18 percent.

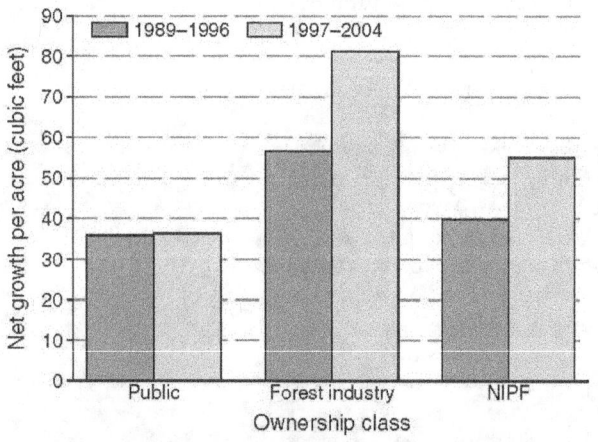

Figure 21—Average annual net growth per acre of softwood live trees in Georgia by ownership class and survey period (NIPF = nonindustrial private forest).

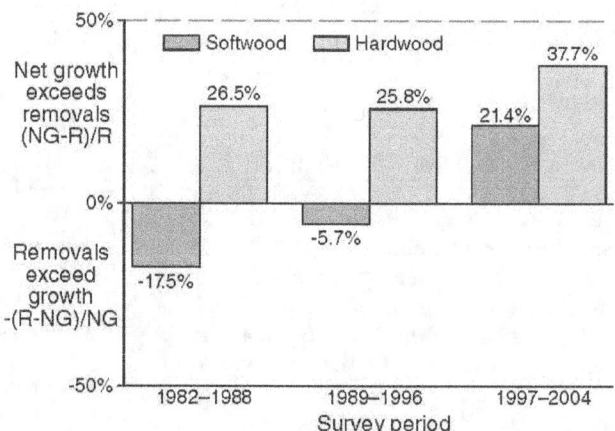

Figure 22—Percent increase and decrease relationship of net growth and removals for live trees in Georgia by survey period.

Hardwood Average Annual Net Growth, Removals, and Mortality

For the last four decades, hardwood average annual net growth of live trees exceeded removals. Net growth of hardwood live trees averaged 625 million cubic feet annually between 1997 and 2004. That is an increase of 14 percent since the last survey. Removals averaged 454 million cubic feet reflecting a 4-percent increase since the 1997 survey. The net change shows that net growth exceeded removals by almost 38 percent. Overall, both net growth and removals have increased during the last three surveys, with net growth outpacing removals by 26 to 38 percent (figs. 22 and 23).

Since 1997, hardwood net growth increased in all the major ownership classes except other public land where growth declined 25 percent. The majority of growth occurred on forest industry land showing an increase of 33 percent, which added more than 19 million cubic feet annually. On NIPF and national forest land, growth increased 15 and 8 percent, respectively. Average annual removals increased 13 percent on NIPF land

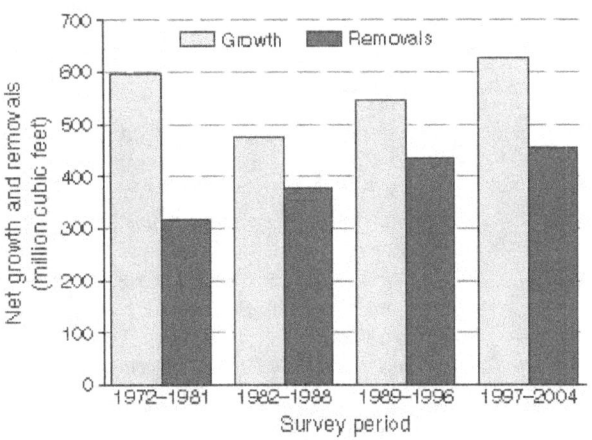

Figure 23—Average annual net growth and removals for hardwood live trees in Georgia by survey period.

removing an additional 42 million cubic feet annually, while forest industry removals only increased 1 percent. Average annual removals declined 27 percent on other public land. Comparable to its softwood removals trend, national forest land also experienced a historic decline in average annual hardwood removals from 19.4 to 0.18 million cubic feet.

Mixed hardwood stand. (photo courtesy of the Georgia Forestry Commission)

25

Average annual removals for this survey ranged from 51 to 72 million cubic feet for each of the 6- through 16-inch diameter classes, accounting for 77 percent of the total removals. The greatest increase in removals occurred in the 12- and 16-inch diameter classes, up 17 and 15 percent, respectively. The remaining smaller diameter classes each experienced an increase of 4 percent or less, except for the 10-inch class which declined 1 percent. Removals in diameter classes > 16 inches declined during this survey period.

The inventory volume for hardwood slightly exceeds softwood volume. However, the average annual net growth for hardwood represents 31 percent of all net growth in Georgia and the average annual removals for hardwood are 28 percent of all removals.

Hardwood mortality experienced a 12-percent decline for 2004. The largest decline was in the Southeast and North Central Survey Units with 23 and 39 percent, respectively. The remaining units each experienced an increased mortality of < 5 percent.

Assessment of productivity of hardwood average annual net growth per acre demonstrates a slightly different trend than softwood and a lower average growth per acre. Total hardwood net growth per acre increased from almost 19 cubic feet in 1989 to 23 cubic feet in 1997 to 26 cubic feet per acre per year in 2004. This marks an increase of almost 14 percent since 1997. Annual net growth per acre by broad ownerships

showed a 60-percent increase on forest industry, while NIPF experienced an 8-percent increase. Hardwood productivity on all public lands declined 17 percent (fig. 24).

This discussion regarding components of change in volume of live trees on timberland in Georgia reflects a positive trend on a broad scale. Softwood has changed from a deficit where removals exceeded growth by 17 percent in the 1980s to a 21-percent surplus of net growth exceeding removals. Hardwood net growth has continued its trend to outpace removals by 38 percent for this survey period.

The relationship of the components of change linked together with a relatively stable timberland area and a peak in total volume demonstrate the effectiveness of sound forest silvicultural methods and reforestation incentives. These forest management efforts by landowners and the forest community, combined with various incentive programs and education, continue to support long-term wood supply for forest products and provide multiple-use benefits from Georgia's vital forest resource.

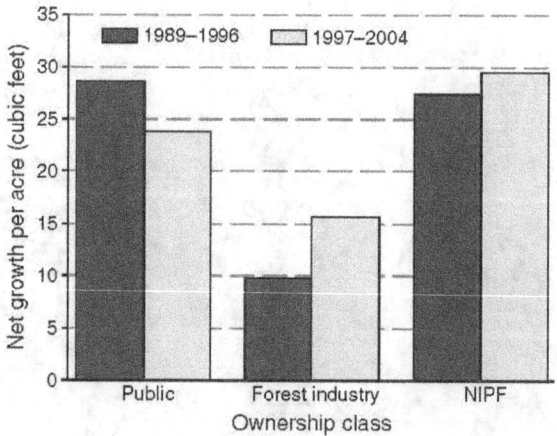

Figure 24—Average annual net growth per acre of hardwood live trees in Georgia by ownership class and survey periods (NIPF = nonindustrial private forest).

Forest Disturbance

Timberland disturbance is part of the dynamics of a forest and can be separated into two categories: forest management treatments and forest disturbances. Forest treatments are part of the forest operations management tools or silvicultural methods such as various harvesting systems, site preparation for establishing a new forest, tree planting, and natural regeneration. Forest disturbances include insect, disease, fire, weather, animal, grazing, and human disturbance such as land clearing. Forest treatments and disturbances are expressed as average annual area or volume estimates for the survey time period.

Forest Management Treatments

Some form of harvesting or timber stand improvement occurred on almost 860,000 acres annually between 1997 and 2004. This represents about 3.5 percent of the timberland area per year. Final harvests averaged about 430,000 acres each year during this survey or < 1.8 percent of all timberland (fig. 25). Each year about 199,000 acres were thinned and 161,000 acres were partially harvested, accounting for a combined 1.5 percent of all timberland. Almost 70,000 acres received some type of other stand improvement. These harvest and management activities resulted in annual removals of live-tree volume averaging 1.6 billion cubic feet since 1997, or 4.4 percent of total live-tree inventory volume.

Properly maintained roads offer multiple environmental benefits. (photo courtesy of the Georgia Forestry Commission)

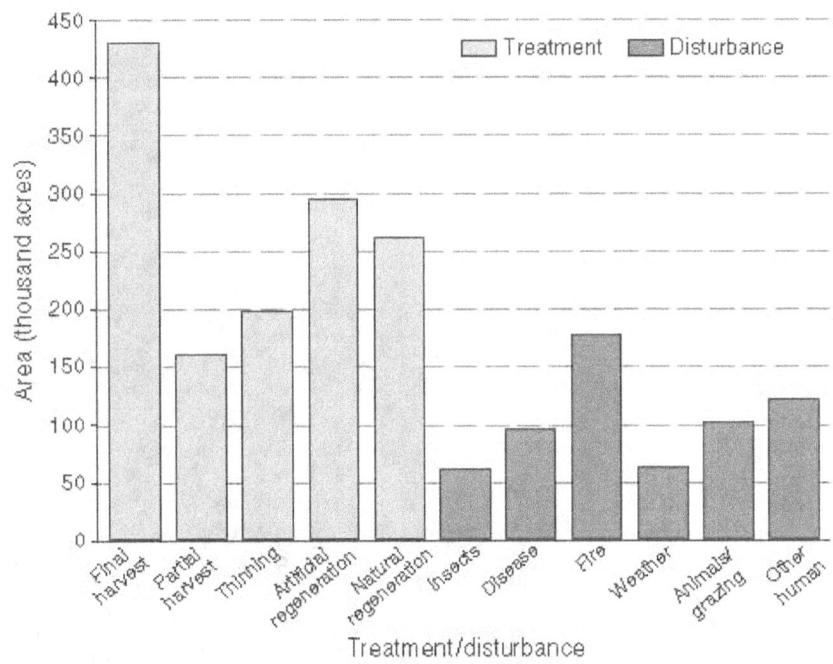

Figure 25—Average area treated/disturbed annually by treatment and disturbance types, Georgia, 1997–2004.

Artificial regeneration (tree planting and direct seeding) occurred on 295,000 acres each year and natural regeneration averaged about 261,000 acres each year. The combined forest regeneration represents about 2.3 percent of the total timberland area each year.

Natural Disturbances

Most disturbances are natural occurrences and have greatly contributed to forest dynamics throughout history. Quite often, disturbances affect small areas and contribute to species richness. However, some large-scale disturbances such as hurricanes, intense fires, or epidemic insect and disease outbreaks can be catastrophic.

From 1997 to 2004, fire contributed to the largest area of natural disturbance across Georgia, and has had the most influence on plant ecology over time. On average, disturbance from wildfire occurred on 178,000 acres each year for the 2004 survey (fig. 25). Natural disturbances from insects and diseases annually affected 61,000 and 96,000 acres, respectively. Periodic cycles of infestation by the SPB have the greatest economic impact on commercial pine timber species. SPB and diseases will be discussed in more detail below. Human-caused disturbances usually include a land clearing activity not associated with a silvicultural activity. These disturbances occurred on about 122,000 acres annually.

Disturbance categories are nonadditive because multiple disturbances may occur on the same acre within a survey cycle, i.e., insect damage may occur after fire or weather events. The total for each disturbance category represents < 1 percent of the total timberland area.

Wildfire is a major component of forest disturbance. (photo courtesy of the Georgia Forestry Commission)

Family Forest Ownership

FIA data were used in conjunction with the National Woodland Owner Survey (NWOS) to compile family forest ownership data (Butler 2007). The NWOS is conducted by the Forest Service in a nationwide effort to identify private forest landowner characteristics, opinions, goals, land management practices, and concerns (Butler and others 2005). While 92 percent of the timberland in Georgia is privately owned, the NWOS focuses on family and individual ownerships which represent about 59 percent of all ownership in Georgia.

FIA and NWOS define timberland ownership as containing 1 acre or more of timberland. The smallest NWOS category of 1 to 9 acres represents 358,000 owners out of the total 525,000 owners in Georgia. The 1- to 9-acres category represents 68 percent of timberland owners, but < 8 percent of the NWOS timberland area or about 4.5 percent of all timberland area. Therefore, the survey answers were compiled for 1 acre and greater, 10 acres and greater, and 50 acres and greater to assess the impact of small timberland parcels (1 to 9 acres) on the results. This disparity of the large number of ownerships to the total acres of timberland appeared to have some influence on certain questions when included. For this reason, the following tables and discussion will focus on timberland ownership of 10 acres or more to offer the perspective of

timberland owners with more opportunity for active forest management. It will be noted where results indicate the 1 acre or greater, or the 50 acres or greater assessments. The survey was conducted from 2002 to 2004 by mail or telephone. There were 643 respondents owning 10 or more timberland acres.

There are about 168,000 timberland family owners in Georgia holding 10 or more acres totaling more than 13 million acres, or about 54 percent of the timberland (table 3). The area drops to 10.8 million acres or 45 percent of the timberland for ownerships ≥ 50 acres.

Foresters assist families to produce healthy, productive forests. (photo courtesy of the Georgia Forestry Commission)

Table 3—Area and number of family-owned forests in Georgia by size of forest landholdings, 2004

Size of forest landholdings	Area			Ownerships			Survey respondents
	Acres	Standard error	Percent	Number	Standard error	Percent	
acres	- - - - thousand - - - -			- - - thousand - - -			count
10–49	2,319	515	17.7	115	12	68.3	115
50–99	1,815	509	13.8	27	3	16.2	90
100–499	4,476	535	34.1	22	2	13.1	222
500–999	1,754	508	13.4	3	<1	1.6	87
1,000–4,999	2,016	511	15.4	1	<1	0.7	100
5,000+	746	491	5.7	<1	<1	<0.1	29
Total	13,126	477	100.0	168	12	100.0	643

Memorable family outings create a legacy and continuity in ownership. (photo courtesy of Big K Farm)

About 41 percent of the owners (≥ 10 acres) have held the timberland for 10 to 24 years, with 23 percent holding the property for 25 to 49 years. Almost 7 percent have owned timberland for 50+ years. These groups control 9.4 million acres of timberland. Almost 6.6 million acres are part of the primary residence for all owners.

Part of the NWOS survey attempts to determine the reasons for timberland ownership, what activities have been conducted, and what activities are planned (table 4). The top five reasons for ownership are:

1. Family legacy
2. Aesthetics
3. Privacy
4. Nature protection
5. Land investment

Timber production ranked 10th and represents 51 percent of the NWOS timberland.

Responses regarding recent forest activities are found in table 5. The top five based on the number of owners were:

1. Private recreation
2. Posting land
3. Road/trail maintenance

4. Timber harvest
5. Tree planting

When ranked by the number of acres in each category, timber harvest ranked second and accounted for almost 47 percent of the NWOS timberland area.

Around 10,000 timberland owners, or 6 percent, have a written management plan, and control more than 2.6 million acres, or 20 percent of the NWOS timberland. Just over 22 percent of the NWOS timberland owners have sought forest management advice representing 6.8 million acres or 52 percent of the NWOS timberland area. The numbers increase for respondents with ≥ 50 acres to 15 percent who have a written plan, and 42 percent sought advice. When adding respondents in the 1- to 9-acre ownership, < 2 percent have a written management plan and only 10 percent sought advice.

Landowners were also asked what might limit their ability to use their woodland or what they believe to be affecting the health of their woodland. The top five concerns facing timberland owners were:

1. Insect/diseases,
2. Property taxes
3. Family legacy (keeping the timberland intact)
4. Fire
5. Trespassing

Fifty-nine percent identified insect and diseases as the greatest threat and 56 percent were concerned about property taxes. Each of these two concerns represented landowners controlling around 8.7 million acres.

Almost 5.3 million acres or 32 percent of family timberland are owned by people at least 65 years old. Landowners between the age of 55 and 64 own 3.3 million acres. Combined, these age classes (55 and older) represent about 65 percent of the family forests in Georgia. About 1 million acres are owned by people younger than 45 years old.

Table 4—Area and number of family-owned forests in Georgia (10+ acres) by reason for owning forest land and ranked by ownerships, 2004

| Reason[a] | Area | | | Ownerships | | | Survey respondents | Ranked |
	Acres	Standard error	Percent	Number	Standard error	Percent	count	acres
	- - - - thousand - - - -			- - - - thousand - - - -				
Family legacy	9,194	532	70	118	10	70	451	1
Aesthetics	8,146	538	62	112	10	67	398	2
Land investment	7,803	539	59	82	8	49	380	3
Nature protection	6,997	541	53	102	10	61	346	4
Privacy	6,755	542	51	111	10	66	335	5
Timber production	6,694	542	51	31	3	18	324	6
Hunting or fishing	6,513	542	50	62	7	37	321	7
Part of farm	5,843	601	45	72	10	43	141	8
Other recreation	3,912	532	30	54	7	32	194	9
Part of home or cabin[b]	3,287	526	25	59	7	35	163	10
Nontimber forest products	1,714	507	13	13	3	8	80	11
Firewood production	726	491	6	9	2	5	36	12
No answer	262	482	2	4	2	2	13	13

Numbers include landowners who ranked each objective as very important (1) or important (2) on a seven-point Likert scale.

[a] Categories are not exclusive.

[b] Includes primary and secondary residences.

Table 5—Area and number of family-owned forests in Georgia (10+ acres) by recent (past 5 years) forestry activity, 2004

| Activity[a] | Area | | | Ownerships | | | Survey respondents |
	Acres	Standard error	Percent	Number	Standard error	Percent	count
	- - - - thousand - - - -			- - - - thousand - - - -			
Private recreation	7,612	599	58.0	77	10	45.8	184
Timber harvest	6,113	554	46.6	37	5	22.0	243
Road/trail maintenance	5,847	541	44.5	41	6	24.4	283
Posting land	5,802	601	44.2	54	9	32.1	140
Tree planting	5,323	539	40.6	36	6	21.4	257
Fire hazard reduction	5,081	539	38.7	33	5	19.6	245
Site preparation	4,637	536	35.3	20	4	11.9	222
Wildlife habitat improvement	4,597	536	35.0	26	4	15.5	221
Application of chemicals	3,992	532	30.4	19	4	11.3	191
Cost share	2,137	513	16.3	7	1	4.2	99
Conservation easement[b]	2,077	188	15.8	15	3	8.9	102
Collection of NTFPs[c]	1,778	514	13.5	16	4	9.5	66
Public recreation	1,234	523	9.4	9	3	5.4	29
Green certification[b]	585	488	4.5	2	1	1.2	28

Numbers in rows and columns may not sum to totals due to rounding.

[a] Categories are not exclusive.

[b] Not limited to past 5 years.

[c] NTFPs = nontimber forest products.

Forest Products and the Economy

Georgia's forest products industry is a vital component of the State's economy. The forest products industry in Georgia ranks second in employee compensation and third in total employees behind food processing industry and textiles (number of employees only) (Riall 2007). It contributes billions of dollars and provides jobs and commerce for the rural counties with minimal increase in urban development. The economic activity generated by forest industry in 2006 included:

Total revenue
   (including multiplier effect) $27.7 billion

Output
   (forestry industry sectors) $17.8 billion
Employee compensation $3.5 billion
Employees   67,733

In 2006, direct activity by forest industry brought $15.5 billion into Georgia and total revenue, with all related and supporting industries, was over $27.7 billion. Each cubic foot of wood harvested and processed in Georgia yields an average of $17 in economic gain. The $27.7 billion associated with the forest products industry includes direct, indirect, and induced effects resulting from the industry operation, i.e., known as the multiplier effect.

Tax revenues generated by Georgia forest industry contributed $580 million to the State budget in 2006. Almost $400 million of this provided State services to forest industry employees, i.e., education, public health, safety and welfare, highways, administration, and other. This yields a net annual revenue of about $180 million to Georgia.

Historical trends show a healthy increase in total economic output of the forest industry in Georgia. However, the total number of jobs generated by forestry and other supporting industries has grown at a lower rate. Figure 26 shows changes in economic activity and employment between 1994 and 2006. During this time period the

Forest products produced in Georgia contributed $17.8 billion in 2006. (SRS photo)

total economic impact of forest industry with supporting industries increased from $13.2 billion to $27.7 billion. Jobs directly and indirectly supporting the industry peaked at over 204,000 in 2001, but declined to 136,000 by 2003. Employment for 2006 rose to 149,000 with an annual compensation of almost $6.8 billion. Although a combination of economic models were used to provide these estimates, the results are reasonable when compared to other economic indices.

For instance, forest production levels increased through the 1990s and then suffered a downturn with the general global economy in late 2001. This resulted from many factors including forest industry consolidation, high U.S. dollar, increased global competition, and high U.S. labor costs (Ince 1999). Competitive pressures from overseas producers and from substitution of alternative materials to replace wood products continues to affect forest products manufacturing in the South, but data showed the industry slowly regaining ground from 2004 through 2006 (Riall 2007). The abundant supply of timber and the weakening of the U.S. dollar in relation to other currencies likely contributed to relative cost reductions leading to forest industry improvements during this time period.

Economic recovery and growth has followed the setback after 2001 with a 40-percent increase in total output of the forest products industry occurring between 2003 and 2006. Although the pulp and paper sector increased less than the industry average at 37 percent, that sector remains the dominant part of the industry with $9.6 billion of output occurring in 2006. The lumber and wood preservation sector improved 43 percent between 2003

and 2006, which is slightly above the industry average. The beginning of a decline in housing and other construction affected several sectors of the industry in the second half of 2006. Figure 27 shows the relative proportion of 2006 economic output of five sectors within the forest industry including: logging and nurseries; lumber and wood preservation; engineered wood, plywood and veneer; pulp and paper; and other secondary processing.

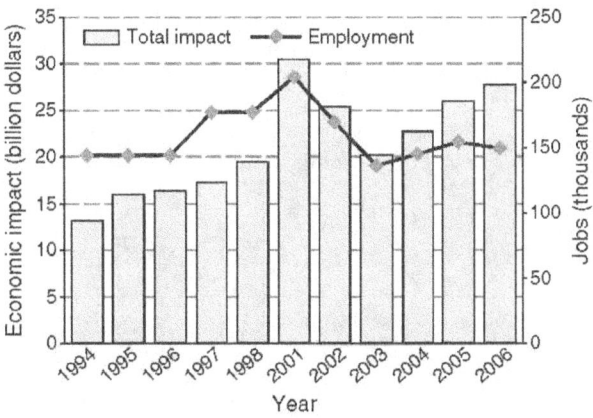

Figure 26—Total economic impact (including multiplier effect) and total employment created by the forest industry in Georgia from 1994 to 2006.

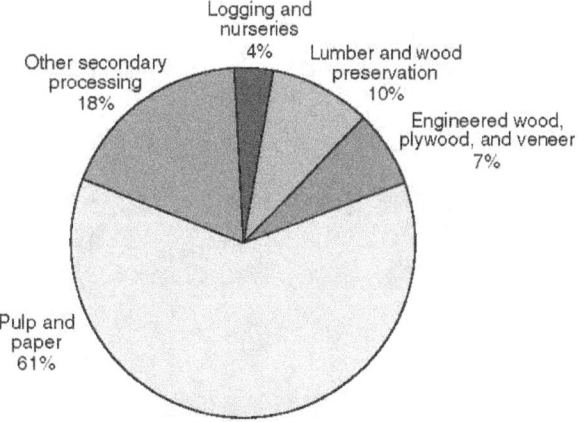

Figure 27—Economic output of forest industry sectors in Georgia, 2006.

Timber Product Output and Removals

In 2005, there were about 181 sawmills, pulpwood mills, and other primary wood-processing plants distributed across the State (fig. 28) (Johnson and others 2007). That year, the total value of shipments for the wood products and paper manufacturing sectors combined contributed more than $15.3 billion to the State's economy (U.S. Department of Commerce 2006). In 1986, there were 301 primary wood-processing mills in Georgia (Tansey and Steppleton 1991). With advances in wood technology and manufacturing, some mills upgraded equipment to be more competitive and improve production. Despite the decline of 201 mills during this period, roundwood production remained at about the same level.

The TPO and removals data come from a questionnaire sent biennially to all primary wood-using mills in Georgia that purchase logs. The survey is conducted in a collaborative effort by the Georgia Forestry Commission (GFC) and the Southern Research Station. The mill survey is conducted to track the types and amounts of roundwood, i.e., saw logs, pulpwood, poles, etc., received by each mill. Additional information was collected about county of origin of the wood, tree species used, and

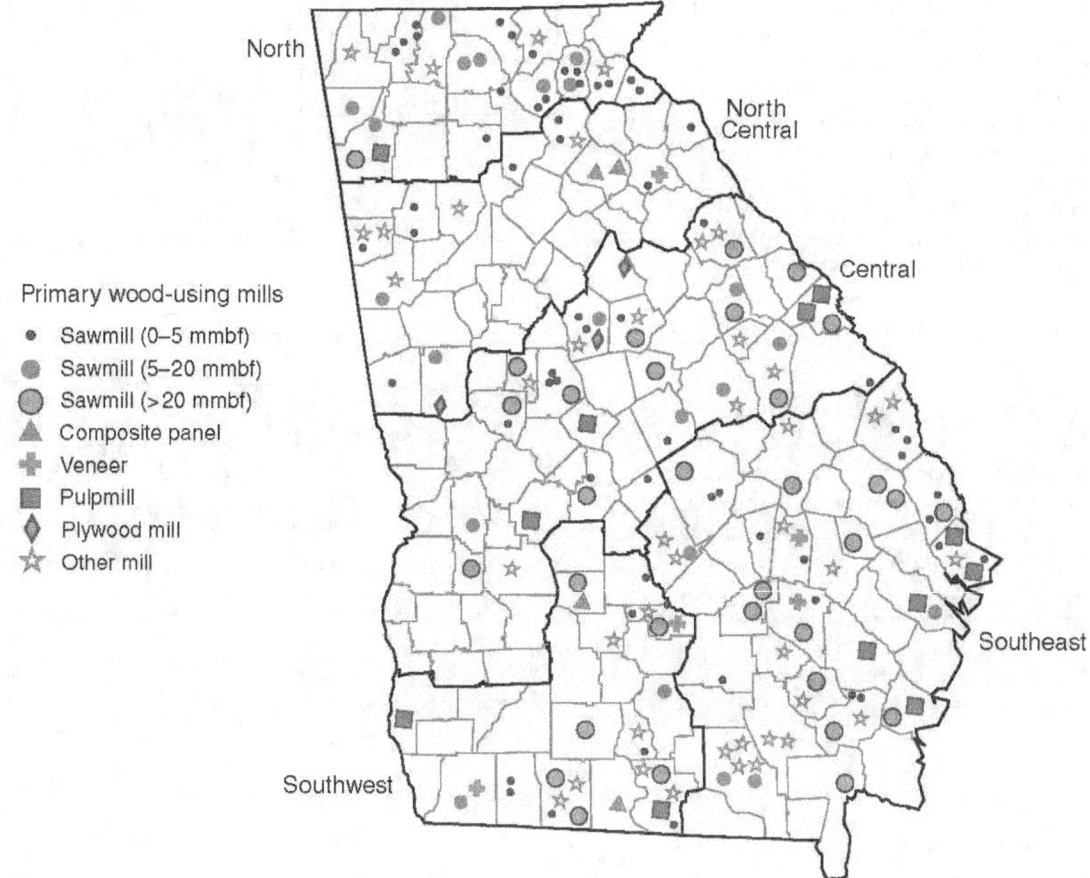

Figure 28—Primary wood-using mills in Georgia, 2005.

how mills use the bark and wood residue produced during processing of logs. For 2005, 92 percent of the mills, accounting for 98 percent of the receipts, responded to the survey. Compiled data represent average production for the years 1997, 1999, 2001, and 2003. Mill data are used to augment the FIA timber removals estimates by identifying the various product proportions by county.

The total output of timber products, which includes domestic fuelwood and plant byproducts, averaged 1.579 billion cubic feet per year between 1997 and 2004 (table 6), which represented a 4-percent decline from the 1989 to 1996 period. Eighty-three percent or 1.307 billion cubic feet of the total output was from roundwood products, while the remainder was from plant byproducts (mill residue). At 1.253 billion cubic feet, softwood species provided 79 percent of the total product output volume. Hardwoods provided the remaining 21 percent, or 326 million cubic feet of total output.

The distribution of total volume among products has remained relatively constant over the past 30 years. Pulpwood has historically been the primary wood product produced by Georgia's mills. Pulpwood production declined nearly 4 percent from 777 million cubic feet in 1996 to 747 million cubic feet for the current survey period (fig. 29). However, pulpwood production accounted for 47 percent of the total TPO volume between 1997 and 2004,

Between 1997 and 2004, almost 1.7 million loads of roundwood came from Georgia timberlands each year. (photo courtesy of Big K Farm)

Less than 1 percent of mill residues are not used as a byproduct. (SRS photo)

Table 6—Average annual output of timber products by product, species group, and type of material, Georgia, 1997 to 2004

Product and species group	Standard units	Total output Number of units	Total output Million cubic feet	Roundwood products Number of units	Roundwood products Million cubic feet	Plant byproducts Number of units	Plant byproducts Million cubic feet
Saw logs	k fbm[a]						
Softwood		2,324,908	439.0	2,304,792	435.3	20,116	3.7
Hardwood		399,127	67.9	389,952	66.3	9,175	1.5
Total		2,724,035	506.8	2,694,744	501.6	29,291	5.2
Veneer logs and bolts	k fbm[a]						
Softwood		350,188	59.1	350,188	59.1	—	—
Hardwood		88,350	14.4	88,350	14.4	—	—
Total		438,538	73.5	438,538	73.5	—	—
Pulpwood[b]	cords[c]						
Softwood		7,757,569	582.2	5,828,362	442.2	1,929,207	140.0
Hardwood		2,193,276	165.3	1,951,410	147.1	241,866	18.1
Total		9,950,845	747.4	7,779,772	589.3	2,171,073	158.1
Composite panels	cords[c]						
Softwood		1,315,345	97.6	555,152	42.5	760,193	55.2
Hardwood		78,714	5.9	68,621	5.2	10,093	0.8
Total		1,394,059	103.5	623,773	47.6	770,286	55.9
Poles and piling	k pieces						
Softwood		5,713	9.8	5,713	9.8	—	—
Hardwood		—	—	—	—	—	—
Total		5,713	9.8	5,713	9.8	—	—
Posts (round and split)	k pieces						
Softwood		3,899	2.5	3,899	2.5	—	—
Hardwood		3,959	—	3,959	—	—	—
Total		7,858	2.5	7,858	2.5	—	—
Other[d]	k ft[3]						
Softwood		51,931	51.9	7,400	7.4	44,531	44.5
Hardwood		6,469	6.5	586	0.6	5,883	5.9
Total		58,400	58.4	7,986	8.0	50,414	50.4
Total industrial products							
Softwood		—	1,242.0	—	998.7	—	243.3
Hardwood		—	259.9	—	233.6	—	26.3
Total		—	1,501.9	—	1,232.2	—	269.7
Fuelwood[e]	cords						
Softwood		151,181	11.0	140,127	10.2	11,054	0.8
Hardwood		869,418	65.7	858,099	64.8	11,319	0.8
Total		1,020,599	76.6	998,226	75.0	22,373	1.7
All products							
Softwood		—	1,253.0	—	1,008.9	—	244.1
Hardwood		—	325.5	—	298.4	—	27.2
Total		—	1,578.5	—	1,307.2	—	271.3

Numbers in rows and columns may not sum to totals due to rounding.
— = no sample for the cell.
[a] International ¼-inch rule.
[b] Roundwood figures include an estimated 15.5 million cubic feet of roundwood chipped at other primary wood-using plants.
[c] Roughwood basis (includes chips converted to equivalent standard cords).
[d] Includes litter, mulch, particleboard, charcoal, and other specialty products.
[e] Excludes approximately 72.4 million cubic feet of wood residues and 108.5 million cubic feet of bark used for industrial fuel.

the same as the time period of 1989 to 1996. This compares to a 50-percent share between 1982 to 1988, 52 percent between 1972 to 1981, and 58 percent between 1961 to 1971. Since 1997, softwood pulpwood production was down 1.8 million cubic feet to 582 million cubic feet, while hardwood pulpwood production declined nearly 28 million cubic feet, or 14 percent, to 165 million cubic feet. Softwood accounted for 78 percent of the total pulpwood production in 2004. Plant byproducts or mill residue of total softwood and hardwood pulpwood production accounted for 24 and 11 percent, respectively. The 158 million cubic feet of plant byproducts used for pulpwood production accounted for 58 percent of mill residue utilized for products (table 6).

Saw-log production, used mainly for dimension lumber, declined 5 percent, from 534 million cubic feet in 1996 to 507 million cubic feet in 2004. Saw-log output accounted for 32 percent of the total TPO volume between 1997 and 2004, about the same as in the last four survey periods.

Veneer-log production was down nearly 4 percent, from 76 to 73 million cubic feet and accounted for 5 percent of the total TPO volume. At 71 million cubic feet, other industrial products—poles and pilings, posts, and other (table 6)—accounted for 4 percent of total product output. Industrial products accounted for 95 percent of the State's total product output. Composite panel production increased nearly 14 percent, from 91 to 104 million cubic feet and represented 7 percent of the total TPO volume.

Domestic fuelwood declined 33 percent to 77 million cubic feet, but still accounted for 5 percent of total product output for the State. The mill residue used for industrial fuel amounted to 181 million cubic feet and accounted for 40 percent of the utilized mill byproducts. It should be noted that domestic fuelwood for this survey period is taken from the U.S. Department of Energy data and should not be used to infer accurate trends with historical fuelwood TPO data.

Log skidder. (photo courtesy of the Georgia Forestry Commission)

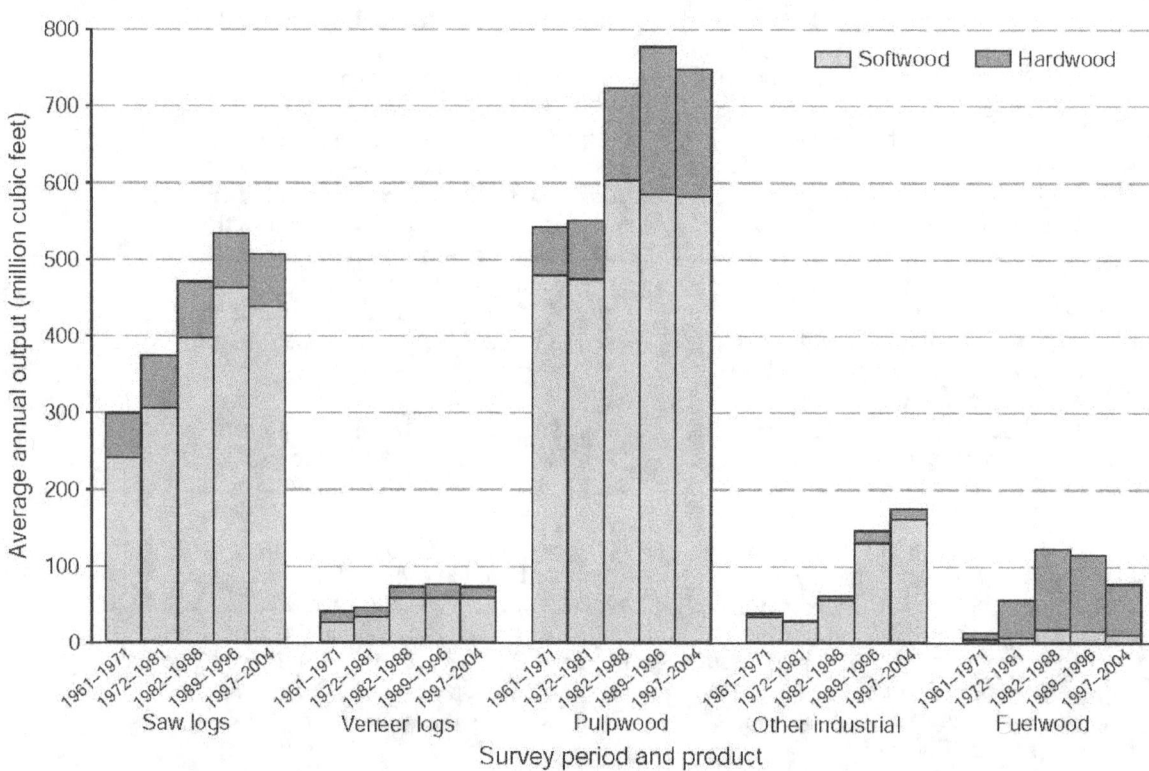

Figure 29—Average annual output of timber products by survey period, product, and species group, Georgia, 1971 to 2004.

Average annual output of roundwood products (including fuelwood) was down 6 percent, or 82 million cubic feet, from 1.389 billion cubic feet in the previous FIA survey period, to an average of 1.307 billion cubic feet between 1997 and 2004. Softwood roundwood production declined only 1 percent to 1.009 billion cubic feet, while hardwood roundwood production declined 20 percent to 298 million cubic feet. Roundwood pulpwood and saw-log production amounted to 589 and 502 million cubic feet, respectively. These two products accounted for 83 percent of the total roundwood production for the State. Ninety-six percent of the roundwood products volume came from growing-stock trees, split between sawtimber (68 percent) and poletimber (32 percent) (table 7). The combined other sources, which include cull trees, salvable dead, and stumps and tops

of harvested trees, dropped from 94 million cubic feet reported in the previous survey period to 58 million cubic feet.

Total timber removals, averaged over the time period, are the sum of the volume of roundwood products, logging residues (unused portions of trees left in the woods), and other removals (removals attributed to land clearing or land use changes) from growing stock and nongrowing-stock sources. Removals from all sources, for both softwoods and hardwoods combined, totaled 1.993 billion cubic feet (table 8). Softwoods accounted for 72 percent of total removals. Volume used for roundwood products totaled 1.307 billion cubic feet, or 65 percent, of total removals. Logging residues and other removals amounted to 452 million cubic feet (23 percent) and 234 million cubic feet (12 percent), respectively.

Table 7—Average annual output of roundwood products by product, species group, and source of material, Georgia, 1997 to 2004

Product and species group	All sources	Growing-stock trees			Cull trees[a]	Salvable dead trees[a]	Other sources[b]
		Total	Sawtimber	Poletimber			
			million cubic feet				
Saw logs							
Softwood	435.3	426.1	401.5	24.6	0.3	0.1	8.7
Hardwood	66.3	64.9	61.1	3.8	0.1	0.2	1.2
Total	501.6	491.0	462.6	28.4	0.4	0.3	9.9
Veneer logs and bolts							
Softwood	59.1	57.9	57.3	0.6	—	—	1.2
Hardwood	14.4	14.2	14.1	0.1	—	0.0	0.2
Total	73.5	72.1	71.3	0.8	—	0.0	1.4
Pulpwood							
Softwood	442.2	429.7	182.8	246.9	2.0	0.1	10.4
Hardwood	147.1	135.2	49.9	85.3	3.6	0.3	8.1
Total	589.3	564.9	232.8	332.1	5.6	0.4	18.4
Composite panels							
Softwood	42.5	40.8	16.7	24.1	0.5	—	1.1
Hardwood	5.2	4.7	1.9	2.8	0.2	—	0.2
Total	47.6	45.5	18.6	26.9	0.7	—	1.4
Poles and piling							
Softwood	9.8	9.5	9.5	—	—	0.0	0.2
Hardwood	—	—	—	—	—	—	—
Total	9.8	9.5	9.5	—	—	0.0	0.2
Posts (round and split)							
Softwood	2.5	2.4	1.7	0.7	0.0	—	0.0
Hardwood	—	—	—	—	—	—	—
Total	2.5	2.4	1.7	0.7	0.0	—	0.0
Other							
Softwood	7.4	7.2	4.2	3.0	0.0	0.0	0.1
Hardwood	0.6	0.5	0.3	0.2	0.0	0.0	0.0
Total	8.0	7.7	4.5	3.2	0.1	0.1	0.1
Total industrial products							
Softwood	998.7	973.7	673.8	300.0	2.9	0.3	21.8
Hardwood	233.6	219.5	127.3	92.2	3.9	0.5	9.7
Total	1,232.2	1,193.2	801.1	392.2	6.8	0.7	31.5
Fuelwood							
Softwood	10.2	7.3	5.1	2.2	0.5	0.1	2.3
Hardwood	64.8	48.6	37.3	11.3	2.3	0.7	13.2
Total	75.0	55.9	42.4	13.5	2.8	0.8	15.5
All products							
Softwood	1,008.9	981.1	678.9	302.2	3.4	0.4	24.0
Hardwood	298.4	268.1	164.6	103.5	6.2	1.1	22.9
Total	1,307.2	1,249.2	843.5	405.7	9.6	1.5	47.0

Numbers in rows and columns may not sum to totals due to rounding.
— = no sample for the cell; 0.0 = a value of > 0.0 but < 0.05 for the cell.
[a] On timberland.
[b] Includes trees < 5.0 inches in diameter, tree tops and limbs from timberland, or material from other forest land or nonforest land such as fence rows or suburban areas.

Forest harvesting. (SRS photo)

Table 8—Volume of timber removals by removals class, species group, and source, Georgia, 1997 to 2004

Removals class and species group	All sources	Source Growing stock	Nongrowing stock
		million cubic feet	
Roundwood products			
Softwood	1,008.9	981.1	27.8
Hardwood	298.4	268.1	30.2
Total	1,307.2	1,249.2	58.0
Logging residues			
Softwood	295.9	77.6	218.3
Hardwood	155.9	76.6	79.3
Total	451.8	154.2	297.6
Other removals			
Softwood	122.3	95.7	26.6
Hardwood	111.8	74.2	37.6
Total	234.0	169.8	64.2
Total removals			
Softwood	1,427.0	1,154.3	272.7
Hardwood	566.1	418.9	147.1
Total	1,993.1	1,573.2	419.9

Numbers in rows and columns may not sum to totals due to rounding.

Nontimber Forest Products

Georgia has an active and vibrant industry based on collection of NTFPs. These products originate from fungi, moss, lichen, herbs, vines, shrubs, and trees. They are made from the roots, tubers, leaves, bark, twigs, branches, fruit, and sap, as well as wood that is gathered but not cut from timber. The products are not included in the traditional definition of the forest products industry, but are important components to other industries—herbal medicines, culinary, crafts, floral, and landscaping. They range from edible products (fruits, nuts, mushrooms, ramps, and maple syrup), to medicinal type products (ginseng and bloodroot), to ornamental products (Christmas trees, galax, pine tips for garlands, and grapevines), landscape products (native plants and pine straw), and specialty woods (burl and crotch wood for fine crafts).

A survey of county extension agents was designed to estimate the number and distribution of NTFP enterprises in the Southern United States. Results, based on a response rate of 94 percent, show that Georgia has an estimated 1,974 NTFP firms (Chamberlain 2005, Chamberlain and Predny 2003) as of April 2003. The State ranked fourth behind North Carolina, Kentucky, and Tennessee in total number of NTFP enterprises in the region, accounting for about 8 percent of the regional total (table 9).

Georgia ranked sixth in the South with a total of 68 firms that specialize in products made from medicinal plants, accounting for 1.5 percent of all such enterprises. In the South, Georgia ranked in the top 10 firms for specialty wood products, edible forest products, floral and decorative products,

Pine straw generates the largest nontimber forest product revenue in Georgia. (photo by David J. Moorhead, University of Georgia)

Table 9—Total number and distribution of NTFP enterprises in the Southern United States as perceived by county extension agents

State	Edible	Specialty wood	Floral and decorative	Landscape	Medicinal	Total	Percent of total
			------- number -------				
Alabama	221	377	378	377	58	1,411	6
Arkansas	224	257	208	120	251	1,060	4
Florida	216	127	182	837	50	1,412	6
Georgia	250	186	384	1,086	68	1,974	8
Kentucky	490	826	562	373	2,670	4,921	19
Louisiana	249	119	94	81	8	551	2
Mississippi	234	252	207	192	15	900	4
North Carolina	526	452	3,283	1,326	770	6,357	25
Oklahoma	275	148	75	65	14	577	2
South Carolina	89	81	145	216	25	556	2
Tennessee	390	794	481	593	314	2,572	10
Texas	438	210	200	196	27	1,071	4
Virginia	239	370	698	376	262	1,945	8
Total	3,841	4,199	6,897	5,838	4,532	25,307	
Percent of total	15	17	27	23	18		

NTFP = nontimber forest product.

wild-harvested materials and native plants, and plants collected from the wild for landscaping.

Survey results revealed that Georgia has a widely distributed and diverse array of enterprises that use nontimber forest resources to manufacture products (fig. 30). About 3.4 percent of the NTFP enterprises deal with medicinal plants. Another 9 percent manufacture specialty wood products and about 13 percent manufacture culinary items from forest harvested resources. Floral and decorative enterprises account for 19.5 percent of Georgia's NTFP industry. Landscaping firms that use native plants or plants collected from the wild, account for about 55 percent of the industry in the State.

Georgia, with its diverse ecosystems and large urban populations has a distinct distribution of major NTFP. The northern region of the State is the prime supplier of ginseng. Ten counties on the northern border of the State report harvesting of this important medicinal plant. Most of the major suppliers of Christmas trees are located near metropolitan Atlanta. The major pine straw producers are in the southeast Georgia pine forest region. These three products represent diverse market segments (medicinal, floral, and landscape) that contribute to Georgia's economy.

The value of some NTFPs makes an important contribution to local economies in Georgia. The following estimates represent a 5-year average from 2001

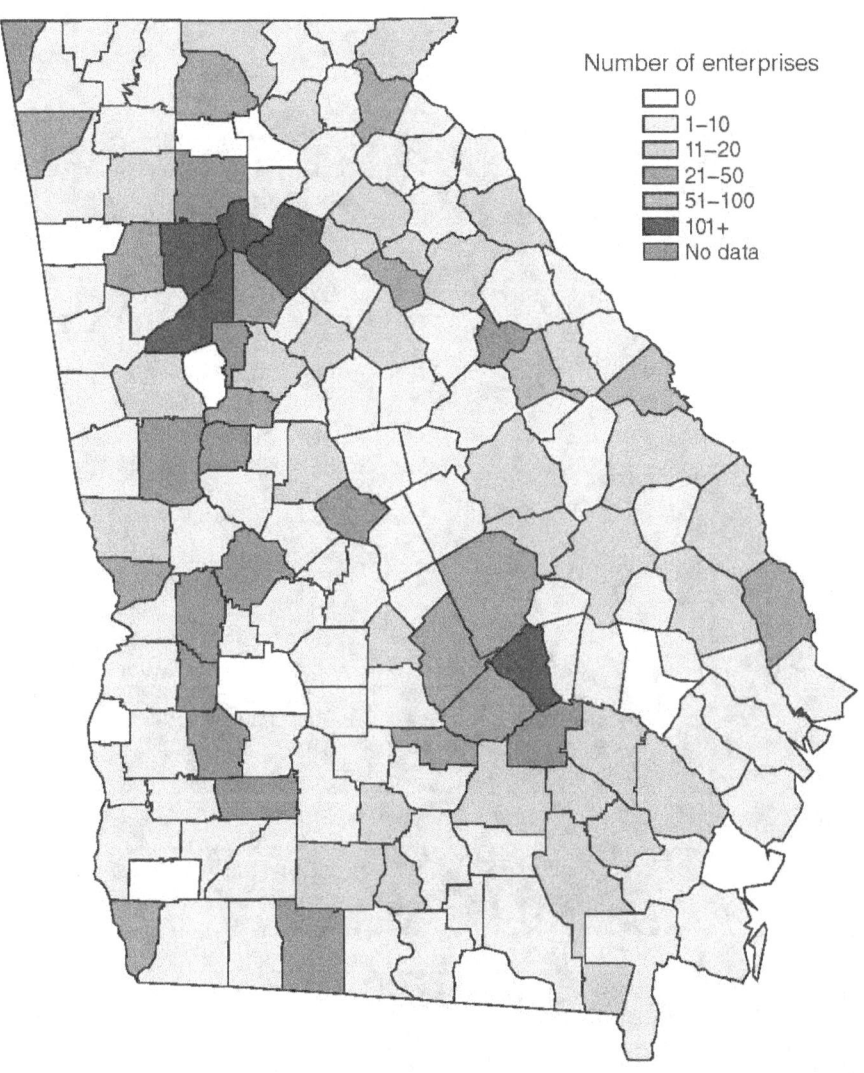

Figure 30—Estimated distribution of nontimber forest products enterprises, Georgia, 2004.

to 2005 as reported from the University of Georgia, College of Agricultural and Environmental Sciences "Georgia Farm Gate Value Report" (Boatright and McKissick 2003, 2004, 2005, 2006, 2007):

Christmas trees	$9.2 million
Pine straw	$26.5 million

The evidence presented provides a look at the majority of the NTFP industry in Georgia. Other products, such as saw palmetto, sphagnum moss, and native plants, are known to be collected from Georgia's forests, but data on the volumes and values were not readily available. Overall, the available NTFP data reveals the industry provides a niche in the Georgia economy.

Water Quality and Best Management Practices

Contained within Georgia's 24.2 million acres of commercial timberland are 69,000 miles of perennial and intermittent streams and canals. The headwaters of the streams, rivers, and lakes provide the foundation for ecological diversity and varied wildlife habitats, and general quality of life. Assurance of water quality begins with responsible forest practices sanctioned by forest landowners and the forestry community.

Since the promulgation of the 1972 Federal Clean Water Act, the Georgia Environmental Protection Division (GAEPD) has been responsible for managing and protecting waters of the State from point and nonpoint source pollution. According to the 2003 Georgia's environment report by the GAEPD, water quality was assessed along 11,287 miles of streams. Those results indicated that 43 percent of the miles fully support their designated uses while 32 percent partially support them, and 25 percent do not support their designated uses. Water quality impairment along approximately 10 percent of streams is caused by nonpoint pollution sources. Improperly executed forestry practices contribute nonpoint pollution to any stream or water body. Nonpoint pollution from forest practices contributes < 3 percent to State waters (U.S. Environmental Protection Agency 2005).

Since 1977, the GAEPD has designated the GFC as the lead BMP agency, responsible for development, implementation, monitoring, and education. Forestry BMPs were created to avert nonpoint source pollution, particularly erosion and sedimentation. They were developed in 1981 and revised in 1999. The standards, set forth under the Rules and Regulations for Water Quality Control in Georgia, chapter 391–3–6, issued guidance regarding the use of BMPs to meet the turbidity standard. For silvicultural land disturbance activities, the proper design, installation, and maintenance of BMPs shall constitute compliance.

Assessment of implementation and compliance of BMPs is determined through site monitoring surveys and during complaint resolution procedures. Site monitoring surveys provide statistical assessment of whether a forest operation had implemented applicable BMPs, and if applications of the BMPs are in

Harvest using streamside management zones for water quality. (SRS photo)

compliance to effectively protect water quality. The scores, expressed as a percent, are based on the number of survey questions scored in favor of implementation and compliance and divided by the total list of applicable questions. The GFC conducted BMP implementation and compliance surveys in 1991, 1992, 1998, 2002, and 2004.

Figures 31 and 32 demonstrate improvements by forest practice for BMP implementation and compliance, respectively. Since the 1991 survey, the percentage of acres in BMP compliance has increased from 86 to 99.4 percent. BMP implementation has increased from 64.9 to 89.8 percent. The percentage of streams (miles) in compliance has remained around 95 percent. Since the 1998 survey, the number of water quality risks has decreased by 59.6 percent, from 544 to 220 (Georgia Forestry Commission 2005).

By 2004, most scores improved to the 90 to 100 percentile reflecting an acceptable rate of implementation and compliance along with suggestions for further improvement. Roads (construction and location) and stream crossings have been identified as focus areas. Road construction experienced the most improved compliance rising from 69 percent in 1991 to 93 percent by 2004. While the stream crossings category showed improvement, it still remains an area for focused training and monitoring with compliance at 44 percent; however, implementation of stream crossing BMPs was almost 81 percent in 2004.

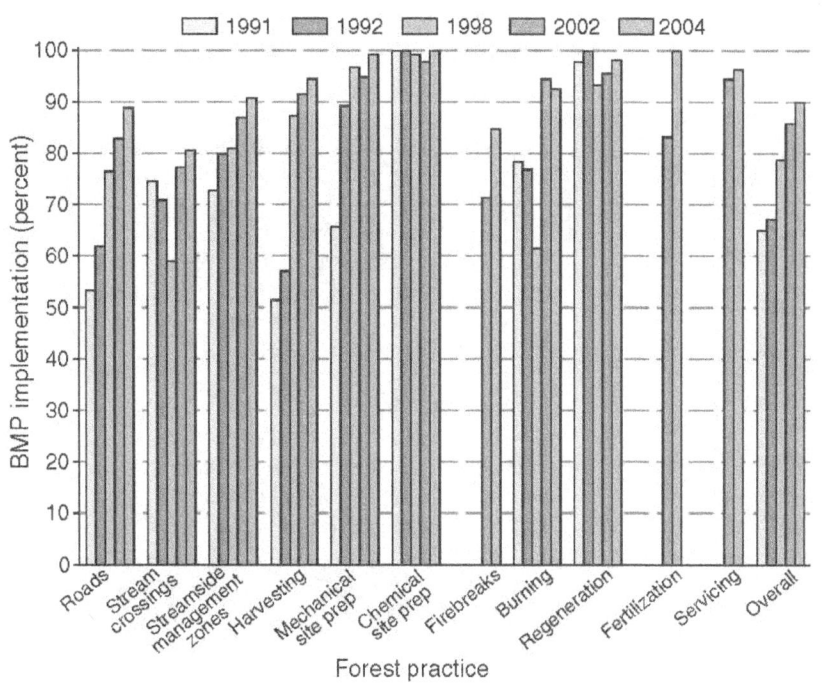

Figure 31—Percent best management practice (BMP) implementation by forest practice and year assessed, Georgia.

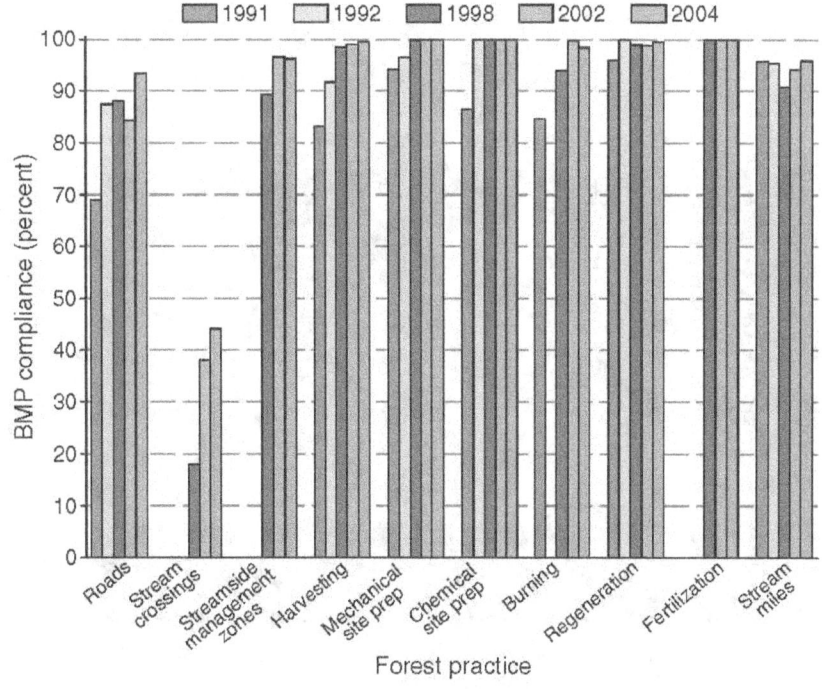

Figure 32—Percent best management practice (BMP) compliance by forest practice and year assessed, Georgia.

45

Forest Health

Insects and Diseases

Georgia's forest land is composed of about 45 percent pine and other softwoods and 55 percent hardwoods with each type having various risks from insects, diseases, environmental stresses, catastrophic events, and other decimating factors. The greatest forest health threat to commercial forestry in Georgia remains the SPB.

During periodic epidemic surges in population, SPB caused catastrophic losses in mostly the north half of the State, but also in some Coastal Plain counties. Epidemic outbreaks occur when one or more SPB infestations can be found per 1,000 acres of host type. Overstocked and overmature stands on eroded Piedmont clay soils, coupled with extended drought and population dynamics of the SPB, caused 57 percent of the counties to experience periodic epidemic SPB outbreaks (fig. 33). SPB losses averaged $7.4 million since 1972, but the worst outbreak occurred in 2002 with an estimated loss of more than $57 million (Georgia Forestry Commission 2007).

The loblolly-shortleaf pine forest type comprises about 7.3 million acres of the softwood forest type and is considered the primary host of this insect. The majority of the remaining pine forest type is comprised of slash and longleaf pine which tend to have a greater natural resistance to SPB attacks. Although some losses from bark beetles do occur in these species, the severity and occurrence is much lower than with loblolly and shortleaf. Federal funding through the Forest Service since 2003 provided a statewide cost-share program allowing private landowners to implement practices that will lower the risk of damage. Examples of preventive treatments include precommercial thinning, release treatments, and prescribed burning.

Other native pests and pathogens that impact Georgia's forests include: annosum root disease; numerous defoliating and terminal feeding insects (such as sawflies,

Aerial view of southern pine beetle progression. (photo courtesy of the Georgia Forestry Commission)

Tree with pitch tubes. (photo by Tim Tigner, Virginia Department of Forestry) and (inset) Southern pine beetle. (photo by Erich G. Vallery, U.S. Forest Service)

twig girdlers, twig borers, and leaf miners); various shoot and stem diseases (such as diplodia tip blight and pitch canker); and needle and foliage diseases (such as needle cast, brown spot needle disease, and powdery mildew). While these cause isolated damage, none have risen to epidemic outbreaks for extended periods of time and the effects of most can be minimized through effective forest management.

Some nonnative species that have historically had an impact on Georgia's forests include chestnut blight, Dutch elm disease, gypsy moth, and Asian ambrosia beetle. In recent years, the hemlock woolly adelgid, the redbay ambrosia beetle, and associated laurel wilt disease complex have had a negative impact on Georgia's forests. As a preventive measure, GFC and other Federal and State agencies are proactively engaged in surveying southern forests for other invasive insects or diseases that occur elsewhere in North America, including the sudden oak death pathogen, sirex woodwasp, emerald ash borer, gypsy moth, and Asian longhorn beetle.

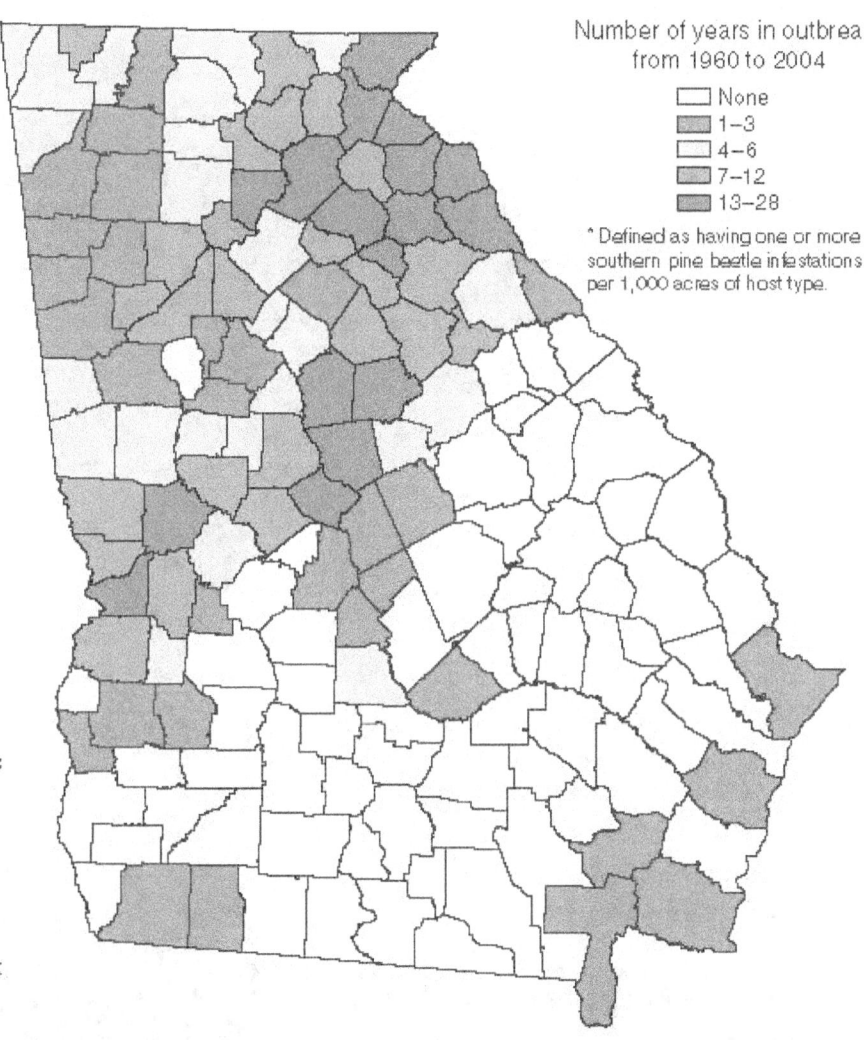

Number of years in outbreak*
from 1960 to 2004

- None
- 1–3
- 4–6
- 7–12
- 13–28

* Defined as having one or more southern pine beetle infestations per 1,000 acres of host type.

Figure 33—Southern pine beetle occurrences in Georgia, 1960 to 2004 (based upon annual aerial surveys conducted by the Georgia Forestry Commission and partially funded by the U.S. Department of Agriculture Forest Service).

Hemlock woody adelgid eggs on hemlock leaves. (photo courtesy of the Georgia Forestry Commission)

Typical strings of compacted sawdust and fross produced by the redbay ambrosia beetle on redbay bark. (photo courtesy of James Johnson, Georgia Forestry Commission)

Thinning or yellowing crowns are the first indication of annosus disease in pine trees. (photo courtesy of James Johnson, Georgia Forestry Commission)

Nonnative Invasive Plant Species

The impact of nonnative invasive plant species to forest land resources continues to be a growing concern as global trade increases. Nonnative species of plants can displace native vegetation and harm our forests through productivity losses and displacement of native plants which may have greater ecological or wildlife value. Prevention offers the best defense from unwanted introductions, followed by a program of early detection and rapid response. Data from FIA plots contribute to early detection as field crews look for 33 nonnative invasive plant species with life forms including trees, shrubs, vines, grasses, ferns, herbs, and other nonwoody species. The data is collected on forested plots only and usually under a forested canopy.

The total cover area for each nonnative invasive species was estimated by summing the expanded area for each infested subplot or subplot condition times the percent cover of each species. The total forest land area covered by nonnative invasive species in Georgia is about 1.27 million acres or 5 percent. This is less than the Southwide average of 9 percent for this survey period.

Out of the 28 species identified on FIA plots in Georgia, 2 species covered over 4.3 percent of all forest land area. Japanese honeysuckle (*Lonicera japonica*) was the most abundant and represented 3 percent of the forest land area. Honeysuckle continues to be sold as an ornamental groundcover and has been a recommended planting for wildlife browse value. Chinese/European privet (*Ligustrum sinense/vulgare*) accounted for 1.4 percent of the cover area, and is considered a greater threat, particularly to lowland forests and along forest edge and fence rows.

Chinese lespedeza (*Lespedeza cuneata*), kudzu (*Pueraria montana* var. *lobata*), and shrubby lespedeza (*L. bicolor*) make up the remaining top five nonnative invasives on forest land and each accounts for about 0.1 percent of the forest land area (table 10).

Kudzu, a nonnative invasive species, is found mostly on forest edge. (photo courtesy of the Georgia Forestry Commission)

Table 10—Estimated area of nonnative invasive species, Georgia, 2004

Species	Acres	Forest land
	thousand	*percent*
Trees		
Tallowtree, popcorntree	7,204	0.03
Tree-of-heaven, ailanthus	272	0.00
Silktree, mimosa	3,567	0.01
Chinaberrytree	23,057	0.09
Princesstree, paulownia	347	0.00
Russian olive	7	0.00
Shrubs		
Chinese/European privet	338,601	1.37
Nonnative roses	5,799	0.02
Japanese privet	8,745	0.04
Bush honeysuckles	3,128	0.01
Autumn olive	1,771	0.01
Sacred bamboo, nandina	191	0.00
Winged burning bush	—	—
Silverthorn, thorny olive	3,380	0.01
Vines		
Japanese honeysuckle	739,406	2.98
Kudzu	26,669	0.11
Chinese/Japanese wisteria	5,045	0.02
Vincas, periwinkles	95	0.00
Climbing yams	3,101	0.01
Winter creeper, climbing euonymus	—	—
Oriental bittersweet	—	—
English ivy	20	0.00
Grasses		
Tall fescue	24,849	0.10
Nepalese browntop	4,061	0.02
Bamboos	2,992	0.01
Cogongrass	—	—
Chinese silvergrass	1,889	0.01
Giant reed	—	—
Fern and forbs		
Chinese lespedeza	31,745	0.13
Japanese climbing fern	9,225	0.04
Shrubby lespedeza	26,646	0.11
Tropical soda apple	598	0.00
Garlic mustard	—	—
Total invasive cover area	1,272,410	5.13
Total forest land area	24,783,744	

— = no sample for the cell; 0.00 = a value of > 0.00 but < 0.05 for the cell.
Source: Personal communication. 2008. J. Miller, Research Ecologist; and E. Chambliss, Forestry Technician. Unpublished data. On file with: U.S. Department of Agriculture Forest Service, Southern Research Station, G.W. Andrews Forestry Sciences Laboratory, 520 Devall Drive, Auburn University, AL 36849.

Pileated woodpecker.
(photo courtesy of
the Georgia Forestry
Commission)

Down Woody Material

Down woody material (DWM) plot data estimates biomass components on the forest floor that include coarse woody debris, fine woody debris, duff, litter, shrubs/herbs, slash piles, and fuel bed depths. For this discussion DWM focuses on fire risks and fuel loading. DWM data can also be used to assess wildlife habitat dynamics (primarily the coarse woody debris), evaluate soil erosion potential, and estimate and monitor carbon pools.

For the 2004 survey, forest fuel loads average 16 tons per acre on forest land in Georgia. Compared to Alabama's average of 16 tons per acre, Florida's average of 31 tons per acre, and South Carolina's average of 20 tons per acre, Georgia's fuel loads are relatively low. Duff and litter comprise the largest portions of DWM, with averages of 6.5 tons of duff per acre and 3.2 tons of litter per acre, followed by averages of 2.7 tons per acre of fine woody materials, 1.7 tons of slash, and 1.4 tons of coarse woody materials (fig. 34).

Fine woody materials (FWM) represent wood pieces with a diameter of < 3 inches, and are of importance in predicting fire hazard. FWMs are broken out in fuel categories of 1-hour fuels, 10-hour fuels, and 100-hour fuels. Comparing the average tons per acre of FWMs in Georgia to the four-State area average (Alabama, Florida, Georgia, and South Carolina), Georgia's average tons per acre is about the same in all categories except the 1-hour fuels where estimates show 9 percent more than the area average tons per acre (fig. 35).

The majority of Georgia's coarse woody materials (90 percent) is small in diameter, and is in intermediate stages of decay. Northern Georgia, particularly the northeastern part of the State, appears to have slightly higher concentrations of DWM than most of the rest of the State. The oak-hickory forest-type group had the highest mean tons per acre of all DWM combined, while oak-gum-cypress and "other" forest-type groups had the lowest tons-per-acre accumulations.

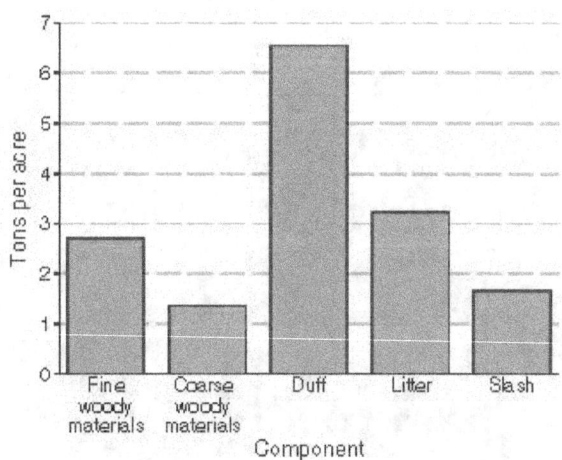

Figure 34—Components of down woody material by volume, Georgia, 2004.

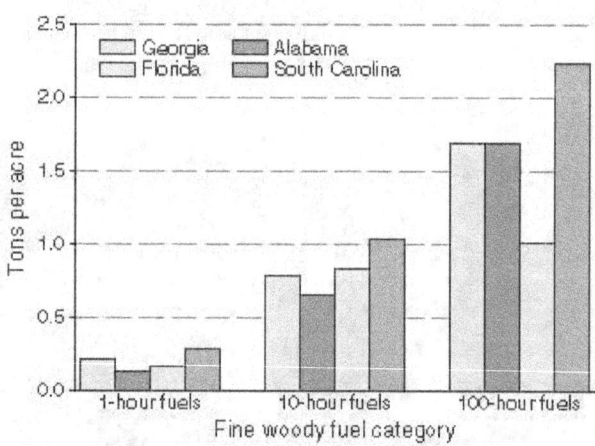

Figure 35—Fine woody fuel categories by State.

On a broad scale for all DWM, the data suggest forest fuels in Georgia have an equal or lower forest fire risk than adjacent States. Higher DWM concentrations in northern Georgia are most likely due to a combination of factors, including land use, topography, and forest type. The humid hardwood forests in north Georgia and in scattered riparian areas are more likely to contribute DWM that is slower to decay and, therefore, accumulate more quickly than pine forests in central and southern Georgia. In addition, pine forests in central and south Georgia are more likely to be managed through use of prescribed burning than oak-pine forests in mountainous north Georgia, which may result in higher amounts of deadwood accumulation on the landscape.

Mixed hardwood stand. (photo courtesy of the Georgia Forestry Commission)

Joseph W. Jones Ecological Research Center at Ichauway, Newton, GA. (photo courtesy of the Georgia Forestry Commission)

Crown Condition

A tree under stress often reacts by slowing growth and shedding parts of its crown (Millers and others 1989). Therefore, negative changes in tree crown condition can be a sign of declining growth rates and degraded forest health. FIA makes visual crown assessments of trees > 4.9 inches d.b.h. to monitor forest health conditions. Relatively high levels of degraded crowns, or negative changes in crown condition over time, indicate areas of concern that may necessitate further investigation. Several indicators have been developed to monitor tree crown condition. These include crown dieback, crown density, and foliage transparency.

For 2000 to 2002 and 2004, crown conditions were assessed on 173 plots across Georgia. Crown conditions recorded during this time have been averaged by species and examined for anomalies that might suggest an underlying forest health problem. Only species with 20 or more observations were summarized individually.

Crown dieback—Crown dieback is a symptom of recent stress, though normal physiological processes may also induce some dieback, e.g., excessive seed production (Millers and others 1992). Crown dieback is recorded as the percent of dead twigs and branches < 1 inch in diameter in the upper and outer portion of the crown. Overall, 91.3 percent of the trees assessed had no crown dieback. Average dieback was 0.2 percent for softwoods and 2.7 percent for hardwoods, and ranged among the individual species from a low of 0.1 percent for slash pine and loblolly pine to a high of 7.2 percent for flowering dogwood (table 11). Light dieback typically occurs more often in hardwoods than in conifers.

Though crown density and foliage transparency are similar measures, they cannot be interpreted as exact inverses. Crown density measures the amount of sunlight blocked by all biomass produced by the tree (both live and dead) in the crown. Foliage transparency measures the amount of sunlight penetrating only the live portion of the crown. Deductions are made from the maximum possible crown density for spaces between branches and other large openings in the crown. However, large gaps in the crown where foliage is not expected to occur are excluded from consideration

Table 11—Mean crown dieback and other statistics for all live trees > 4.9-inches d.b.h., by species, Georgia Inventory (2000 to 2002, 2004)

Species	Plots[a]	Trees	Mean	SE	Minimum	90th percentile	Maximum
	--- number ---		---------------- percent ----------------				
Softwoods							
Slash pine	36	603	0.1	0.0	0	0	25
Loblolly pine	103	1,964	0.1	0.0	0	0	30
Longleaf pine	12	24	0.2	0.2	0	0	5
Eastern white pine	7	35	0.3	0.4	0	0	10
Shortleaf pine	24	94	1.0	0.5	0	0	25
Virginia pine	8	36	2.1	1.5	0	5	50
Other softwoods	21	51	2.5	1.2	0	15	20
All softwoods	143	2,807	0.2	0.1	0	0	50
Hardwoods							
Elm	18	57	1.3	0.5	0	5	10
Yellow-poplar	35	158	1.5	0.5	0	5	50
Hickory	25	52	1.6	0.9	0	5	50
Black cherry	27	42	1.7	0.8	0	5	25
White oaks	46	190	2.5	0.6	0	10	70
Sweetgum	61	217	2.6	0.8	0	5	99
Maple	47	160	2.7	0.9	0	5	95
Tupelo	48	224	2.8	0.9	0	10	99
Red oaks	92	300	3.2	0.9	0	7.5	99
Sweetbay	9	34	3.2	3.1	0	0	99
Other hardwoods	35	110	3.5	1.6	0	7.5	90
Sourwood	11	48	4.0	2.3	0	5	99
Flowering dogwood	15	32	7.2	2.6	0	20	65
All hardwoods	142	1,624	2.7	0.3	0	5	99
All trees	173	4,431	1.1	0.2	0	0	99

The mean, standard error (SE), and median calculations consider the clustering of trees on plots.

[a] Plot totals are not cummulative because multiple species may occur on any given plot.

when foliage transparency is rated. Typically, lower foliage transparency ratings indicate healthy trees, and as with crown density, average foliage transparency tends to be species specific.

Crown density—Crown density is a measure of the amount of foliage present on the tree and is recorded as the percentage of light blocked through the projected crown outline by live and dead branches, foliage, and reproductive structures. Within individual species, greater crown densities typically represent healthy trees. Under normal conditions, average crown densities may vary considerably by species. Most crown densities ranged between 30.0 and 55.0 percent. Average crown density was 39.5 percent for softwoods and 44.3 percent for hardwoods (table 12). Under normal conditions, average crown densities may vary considerably by species since shade tolerance and leaf and branch morphology

affect crown condition. Such differences are present among the species in Georgia. Average crown density ranged from 33.3 percent for Virginia pine to 48.0 percent for yellow-poplar and hickory.

Foliage transparency—Foliage transparency is an indicator of the amount of foliage present on the tree and thus related to growth potential. Foliage transparency is measured as the percent skylight visible through the live, normally foliated portion of the crown. Foliage transparency, like crown density, tends to be species specific. Typically, lower foliage transparency ratings indicate healthy trees. Average foliage transparency was 19.6 percent for all trees combined and ranged

from a low of 15.7 percent for yellow-poplar to a high of 27.5 percent for Virginia pine (table 13).

Overall, average crown conditions in Georgia are similar to the crown condition averages reported by Randolph (2006) for assessments made by the Forest Service, Forest Health Monitoring Program between 1995 and 1999 in six Southern States (Alabama, Georgia, North Carolina, South Carolina, Tennessee, and Virginia). Given the current body of knowledge, the crown condition averages are generally within expected ranges and are not indicative of degraded forest health. One exception may be the crown dieback average for flowering dogwood.

Table 12—Mean crown density and other statistics for all live trees >4.9-inches d.b.h., by species, Georgia inventory (2000 to 2002, 2004)

Species	Plots[a]	Trees	Mean	SE	Minimum	Median	Maximum
	--- number ---		------------------- percent -------------------				
Softwoods							
Eastern white pine	7	35	50.1	1.3	30	50	30
Longleaf pine	12	24	43.5	2.2	30	40	30
Slash pine	36	603	40.3	1.0	5	40	5
Other softwoods	21	51	39.4	2.3	10	40	70
Loblolly pine	103	1,964	39.2	0.9	10	40	10
Shortleaf pine	24	94	38.4	1.1	15	38	15
Virginia pine	8	36	33.3	1.6	10	35	10
All softwoods	143	2,807	39.5	0.7	5	40	70
Hardwoods							
Yellow-poplar	35	158	48.0	1.1	25	50	65
Hickory	25	52	48.0	1.2	20	50	65
White oaks	46	190	45.7	0.9	15	45	65
Black cherry	27	42	45.4	1.8	25	45	65
Red oaks	92	300	45.2	0.8	0	45	75
Sweetgum	61	217	44.3	1.3	0	45	65
Sweetbay	9	34	44.1	2.4	0	48	60
Elm	18	57	43.6	1.2	15	45	65
Maple	47	160	42.9	1.1	10	45	60
Tupelo	48	224	42.5	1.9	0	45	55
Other hardwoods	35	110	41.4	1.5	5	43	65
Flowering dogwood	15	32	40.6	2.3	15	43	60
Sourwood	11	48	40.5	1.8	0	40	55
All hardwoods	142	1,624	44.3	0.5	0	45	75
All trees	173	4,431	41.3	0.5	0	40	75

The mean, standard error (SE), and median calculations consider the clustering of trees on plots.

[a] Plot totals are not cummulative because multiple species may occur on any given plot.

At 7.2 percent, the average dieback for flowering dogwood was relatively high. One possible reason is that dieback is a natural mechanism that allows shaded trees to balance energy reserves (Millers and others 1989), and of the flowering dogwood trees with dieback, 69.2 percent were in the understory and 92.3 percent received either no direct sunlight or direct sunlight on the top or one side of the crown only. Thus, the relatively high dieback levels may be related to the understory habit and shade tolerance of this species. Another possible reason for the relatively high crown dieback average is dogwood anthracnose (*Discula* sp.), a fungus that has been reported in 38 Georgia counties (U.S. Department of Agriculture 2006). Symptoms of anthracnose infection include leaf necrosis and girdling cankers at leaf nodes that cause twig dieback (Mielke and Daughtrey 2006). Just over one-half (56.3 percent) of the dogwoods assessed during this survey were located in counties with confirmed anthracnose occurrence; however, the sample size was too small to perform a valid statistical test for differences in the levels of dieback between dogwoods in counties with and without confirmed anthracnose occurrence. Given that significant mortality due to dogwood anthracnose has been observed in northern Georgia (U.S. Department of Agriculture 2005), data from future surveys should be examined for increased dieback and mortality among the flowering dogwoods.

Table 13—Mean foliage transparency and other statistics for all live trees >4.9-inches d.b.h., by species, Georgia inventory (2000 to 2002, 2004)

Species	Plots[a]	Trees	Mean	SE	Minimum	Median	Maximum
	- - - number - - -		- - - - - - - - - - - - - - - - - percent - - - - - - - - - - - - - - - - -				
Softwoods							
Longleaf pine	12	24	17.9	0.8	15	18	25
Slash pine	36	603	19.4	0.9	10	20	30
Loblolly pine	103	1,964	19.9	0.3	0	20	90
Eastern white pine	7	35	21.0	0.8	15	20	35
Shortleaf pine	24	94	22.5	0.9	0	25	40
Other softwoods	21	51	25.2	5.2	0	20	90
Virginia pine	8	36	27.5	1.4	20	25	55
All softwoods	143	2,807	20.0	0.3	0	20	90
Hardwoods							
Yellow-poplar	35	158	15.7	0.7	10	15	35
Hickory	25	52	16.6	1.1	5	15	40
White oaks	46	190	16.9	0.4	0	15	30
Sweetgum	61	217	17.9	0.8	0	15	99
Flowering dogwood	15	32	18.6	1.5	5	20	30
Black cherry	27	42	19.0	1.3	10	20	35
Elm	18	57	19.3	1.2	10	20	35
Sourwood	11	48	19.4	1.9	15	20	99
Tupelo	48	224	19.6	1.5	10	20	99
Maple	47	160	19.9	1.1	10	20	65
Red oaks	92	300	20.1	0.7	0	20	99
Sweetbay	9	34	20.1	2.8	15	18	99
Other hardwoods	35	110	22.8	1.6	0	20	75
All hardwoods	142	1,624	18.9	0.4	0	20	99
All trees	173	4,431	19.6	0.3	0	20	99

The mean, standard error (SE), and median calculations consider the clustering of trees on plots.
[a] Plot totals are not cummulative because multiple species may occur on any given plot.

Bechtold, W.A.; Patterson, P.L., eds. 2005. The enhanced forest inventory and analysis program—national sampling design and estimation procedures. Gen. Tech. Rep. SRS–80. Asheville, NC: U.S. Department of Agriculture Forest Service, Southern Research Station. 85 p.

Boatright, S.R.; McKissick, J.C. 2003. 2002 Georgia farm gate value report. AR–03–01. Athens, GA: University of Georgia, College of Agricultural and Environmental Sciences. 191 p. http://www.caed.uga.edu/publications/2003/pdf/AR-03-01.pdf. [Date accessed unknown].

Boatright, S.R.; McKissick, J.C. 2004. 2003 Georgia farm gate value report. AR–04–01. Athens, GA: University of Georgia, College of Agricultural and Environmental Sciences. 189 p. http://www.caed.uga.edu/publications/2004/pdf/AR-04-01.pdf. [Date accessed unknown].

Boatright, S.R.; McKissick, J.C. 2005. 2004 Georgia farm gate value report. AR–05–01. Athens, GA: University of Georgia, College of Agricultural and Environmental Sciences. 191 p. http://www.caed.uga.edu/publications/2005/pdf/AR-05-01.pdf. [Date accessed unknown].

Boatright, S.R.; McKissick, J.C. 2006. 2005 Georgia farm gate value report. AR–06–01. Athens, GA: University of Georgia, College of Agricultural and Environmental Sciences. 189 p. http://www.caed.uga.edu/publications/2006/pdf/AR-06-01.pdf. [Date accessed unknown].

Boatright, S.R.; McKissick, J.C. 2007. 2006 Georgia farm gate value report. AR–07–01. Athens, GA: University of Georgia, College of Agricultural and Environmental Sciences. 189 p. http://www.caed.uga.edu/publications/2007/pdf/AR-07-01.pdf. [Date accessed unknown].

Butler, B.J. 2007. Data from the national woodland ownership survey. Unpublished data. On file with: Northeastern Research Station, 11 Campus Boulevard, Newton Square, PA 19073.

Butler, B.J.; Leatherberry, E.C.; Williams, M.S. 2005. Design, implementation, and analysis methods for the national woodland owner survey. Gen. Tech. Rep. NE–336. Newton Square, PA: U.S. Department of Agriculture Forest Service, Northeastern Research Station. 43 p.

Chamberlain, J.L.; Predny, M. 2003. Nontimber forest products enterprises in the South: perceived distribution and implications for sustainable forest management. In: Miller, J.E.; Midtbo, J.M., eds. Proceedings, first national symposium on sustainable natural resource-based alternative enterprises. Mississippi State, MS: Mississippi State University Extension Service and Mississippi State University Forest and Wildlife Research Center: 48–63.

Chamberlain, J. 2005. Nontimber forest products assessment [PowerPoint presentation]. Project summary provided to Forest Inventory and Analysis Research Work Unit, Southern Research Station, 4700 Old Kingston Pike, Knoxville, TN 37919.

Georgia Forestry Commission. 2005. Results of Georgia's 2004 silvicultural best management practices implementation and compliance survey. Macon, GA: Georgia Forestry Commission. 46 p. http://www.gfc.state.ga.us/Resources/documents/SBMPICSurvey2004.pdf. [Date accessed: March 2007].

Georgia Forestry Commission. 2007. Southern pine beetle historical data for Georgia. Macon, GA: Georgia Forestry Commission. 1 p. http://www.gfc.state.ga.us/ForestManagement/documents/SPBHistoricalData2007.pdf. [Date acccessed: March].

Ince, P.J. 1999. Global cycle changes the rules for U.S. pulp and paper. PIMA's North American Papermaker. 81(12): 37–42.

Johnson, T.G.; McClure, N.; Wells, J.L. 2007 Georgia's timber industry—an assessment of timber product output and use, 2005. Resour. Bull. SRS–123. Asheville, NC: U.S. Department of Agriculture Forest Service, Southern Research Station. 36 p.

Knight, H.A.; McClure, J.P. 1974. Georgia's timber. Resour. Bull. SE–27. Asheville, NC: U.S. Department of Agriculture Forest Service, Southeastern Forest Experiment Station. 48 p.

Little, E.L., Jr. 1979. Checklist of United States trees (native and naturalized). Agric. Handb. 541. Washington, DC: U.S. Department of Agriculture. 375 p.

Mielke, M.E.; Daughtrey, M.L. 2006. How to identify and control dogwood anthracnose. NA–GR–18. Radnor, PA: U.S. Department of Agriculture Forest Service, Northern Area State and Private Forestry. http://www.na.fs.fed.us/spfo/pubs/howtos/ht_dogwd/ht_dog.htm. [Date accessed: June].

Millers, I.; Anderson, R.; Burkman, W.; Hoffard, W. 1992. Crown condition rating guide. Newton Square, PA: U.S. Department of Agriculture Forest Service, Northeastern Area State and Private Forestry; Atlanta: U.S. Department of Agriculture Forest Service, Southern Region. 37 p.

Millers, I.; Shriner, D.; Rizzo, D. 1989. History of hardwood decline in the Eastern United States. Gen. Tech. Rep. NE–126. Radnor, PA: U.S. Department of Agriculture Forest Service, Northeastern Forest Experiment Station. 75 p.

Randolph, K. 2006. Descriptive statistics of tree crown condition in the Southern United States and impacts on data analysis and interpretation. Gen. Tech. Rep. SRS–94. Asheville, NC: U.S. Department of Agriculture Forest Service, Southern Research Station. 17 p.

Reams, G.A.; Smith, W.D.; Hansen, M.H. [and others]. 2005. The forest inventory and analysis sampling frame. In: Bechtold, W.A.; Patterson, P.L., eds. The enhanced forest inventory and analysis program—national sampling design and estimation procedures. Gen. Tech. Rep. SRS–80. Asheville, NC: U.S. Department of Agriculture Forest Service, Southern Research Station: 11–26.

Riall, W.B. 2007. Economic benefits of the forestry industry in Georgia: 2006. Atlanta: Enterprise Innovation Institute, Community Policy and Research Services. 28 p.

Sheffield, R.M.; Johnson, T.G. 1993. Georgia's forests, 1989. Resour. Bull. SE–133. Asheville, NC: U.S. Department of Agriculture Forest Service, Southeastern Forest Experiment Station. 97 p.

Sheffield, R.M.; Knight, H.A. 1984. Georgia's forests. Resour. Bull. SE–73. Asheville, NC: U.S. Department of Agriculture Forest Service, Southeastern Forest Experiment Station. 92 p.

Tansey, J.B.; Steppleton, C.D. 1991. Georgia's timber industry—an assessment of timber product output and use. 1989. Resour. Bull. SE–126. Asheville, NC: U.S. Department of Agriculture Forest Service, Southeastern Forest Experiment Station. 23 p.

Thompson, M.T.; Thompson, L.W. 2002. Georgia's forests, 1997. Resour. Bull. SRS–72. Asheville, NC: U.S. Department of Agriculture Forest Service, Southern Research Station. 41 p.

U.S. Department of Agriculture Forest Service. 1992. Forest Service resource inventories: an overview. Washington, DC. 39 p.

U.S. Department of Agriculture Forest Service. 2004a. Forest inventory and analysis national core field guide: field data collection procedures for phase 2 plots. Version 2.0. 208 p. Vol. I. Internal report. On file with: U.S. Department of Agriculture Forest Service, Forest Inventory and Analysis, 201 14th Street, Washington DC 20250.

U.S. Department of Agriculture Forest Service. 2004b. Forest inventory and analysis national core field guide: field data collection procedures for phase 3 plots. Version 2.0. 164 p. Vol. II. Internal report. On file with: U.S. Department of Agriculture Forest Service, Forest Inventory and Analysis, 201 14th Street, Washington DC 20250.

U.S. Department of Agriculture Forest Service. 2005. Georgia forest health highlights 2004. Atlanta: U.S. Department of Agriculture Forest Service, Forest Health Protection, Southern Region. http://www.fs.fed.us/ r8/foresthealth/cooperators/states/fh_ highlights/2004/2004_Georgia.htm. [Date accessed: July 2006].

U.S. Department of Agriculture Forest Service. 2006. Dogwood anthracnose. Atlanta: U.S. Department of Agriculture Forest Service, Forest Health Protection, Southern Region. http://www.fs.fed.us/ r8/foresthealth/atlas/da/da_intro.shtml. [Date accessed: July].

U.S. Department of Agriculture Forest Service. Unpublished data. Washington, DC: State and Private Forestry, Cooperative Forestry.

U.S. Department of Commerce, Bureau of the Census. 2007. Population estimates for the 100 fastest growing counties with 10,000 or more population in 2006: April 1, 2006 to July 1, 2006. [Table 8]. http:// www.census.gov/popest/counties/CO-EST2006-08.html. [Date accessed: May].

U.S. Department of Commerce, Bureau of the Census. 2006. Geographic area statistics, annual survey of manufacturers, 2006. Statistics for the United States and States by industry group: 2005 and 2004. [Table 2]. http://www.census.gov/ prod/2006pubs/am0531as1.pdf. [Date accessed: May].

U.S. Environmental Protection Agency, Office of Water. 2005. National management measures to control nonpoint source pollution from forestry. EPA–841–B–05–001. Washington, DC. 276 p.

Vickery, B.W.; Germain, R.H.; Bevilacqua, E.D. 2009. Urbanization's impact on sustained yield management as perceived by forestry professionals in central New York. Forest Policy and Economics. 11:42–49.

Wear, D.N.; Liu, R.; Foreman, J.M.; Sheffield, R.M. 1999. The effects of population growth on timber management and inventories in Virginia. Forest Ecology and Management. 118: 107–115.

Afforestation. Area of land previously classified as nonforest that is converted to forest by planting trees or by natural reversion to forest.

Average annual mortality. Average annual volume of trees ≥ 5.0 inches d.b.h. that died from natural causes during the intersurvey period.

Average annual removals. Average annual volume of trees ≥ 5.0 inches d.b.h. removed from the inventory by harvesting, cultural operations (such as timber-stand improvement), land clearing, or changes in land use during the intersurvey period.

Average net annual growth. Average annual net change in volume of trees ≥ 5.0 inches d.b.h. in the absence of cutting (gross growth minus mortality) during the intersurvey period.

Basal area. The area in square feet of the cross section at breast height of a single tree or of all the trees in a stand, usually expressed in square feet per acre.

Biomass. The aboveground fresh weight of solid wood and bark in live trees ≥ 1.0 inch d.b.h. from the ground to the tip of the tree. All foliage is excluded. The weight of wood and bark in lateral limbs, secondary limbs, and twigs < 0.5 inch in diameter at the point of occurrence on sapling-size trees is included but is excluded on poletimber and sawtimber-size trees.

Blind check. A reinstallation done by a qualified inspection crew without production crew data on hand; a full reinstallation of the plot is recommended for the purpose of obtaining a measure of data quality. If a full plot reinstallation is not possible, then it is strongly recommended that at least two full subplots be completely remeasured along with all the plot level information. The two datasets are maintained separately. Discrepancies between the two sets of data are not reconciled. Blind checks are done on production plots only. This procedure provides a QA and evaluation function. The statistics band recommends a random subset of plots be chosen for remeasurement.

Bole. That portion of a tree between a 1-foot stump and a 4-inch top d.o.b. in trees ≥ 5.0 inches d.b.h.

Census water. Streams, sloughs, estuaries, canals, and other moving bodies of water ≥ 200 feet wide, and lakes, reservoirs, ponds, and other permanent bodies of water ≥ 4.5 acres in area.

Pine tops are often a residue from logging. (photo courtesy of the Georgia Forestry Commission)

Cold check. An inspection done either as part of the training process, or as part of the ongoing quality control (QC) program. Normally the installation crew is not present at the time of inspection. The inspector has the completed data in-hand at the time of inspection. The inspection can include the whole plot or a subset of the plot. Data errors are corrected. Cold checks are done on production plots only. This type of QC measurement is a "blind" measurement in that the crews do not know when or which of their plots will be remeasured by the inspection crew and cannot, therefore, alter their performance because of knowledge that the plot is a quality assurance (QA) plot.

Compacted area. Type of compaction measured as part of the soil indicator. Examples include the junction areas of skid trails, landing areas, work areas, etc.

Condition class. The combination of discrete landscape and forest attributes that identify and define, and stratify the area associated with a plot. Examples of such attributes include condition status, forest type, stand origin, stand size, owner group, reserve status, and stand density.

Crown. The part of a tree or woody plant bearing live branches or foliage.

Crown density. The amount of crown stem, branches, twigs, shoots, buds, foliage, and reproductive structures that block light penetration through the visible crown. Dead branches and dead tops are part of the crown. Live and dead branches below the live crown base are excluded. Broken or missing tops are visually reconstructed when forming this crown outline by comparing outlines of adjacent healthy trees of the same species and d.b.h.

Crown dieback. This is recent mortality of branches with fine twigs, which begins at the terminal portion of a branch and proceeds toward the trunk. Dieback is only considered when it occurs in the upper and outer portions of the tree. When whole branches are dead in the upper crown, without obvious signs of damage such as breaks or animal injury, assume that the branches died from the terminal portion of the branch. Dead branches in the lower portion of the live crown are assumed to have died from competition and shading. Dead branches in the lower live crown are not considered as part of crown dieback, unless there is continuous dieback from the upper and outer crown down to those branches.

D.b.h. Tree diameter in inches (outside bark) at breast height (4.5 feet aboveground).

Decay class. Qualitative assessment of stage of decay (five classes) of coarse woody debris based on visual assessments of color of wood, presence/absence of twigs and branches, texture of rotten portions, and structural integrity.

Diameter class. A classification of trees based on tree d.b.h. Two-inch diameter classes are commonly used by Forest Inventory and Analysis, with the even inch as the approximate midpoint for a class. For example, the 6-inch class includes trees 5.0 through 6.9 inches d.b.h.

D.o.b. (diameter outside bark). Stem diameter including bark.

Down woody material (DWM). Woody pieces of trees and shrubs that have been uprooted (no longer supporting growth) or severed from their root system, not self-supporting, and are lying on the ground. Previously named down woody debris (DWD).

Duff. A soil layer dominated by organic material derived from the decomposition of plant and animal litter and deposited on either an organic or a mineral surface. This layer is distinguished from the litter layer in that the original organic material has undergone sufficient decomposition that the source of this material, e.g., individual plant parts, can no longer be identified.

Erosion. The wearing away of the land surface by running water, wind, ice, or other geological agents.

Foliage transparency. The amount of skylight visible through microholes in the live portion of the crown, i.e., where you see foliage, normal or damaged, or remnants of its recent presence. Recently defoliated branches are included in foliage transparency measurements. Macroholes are excluded unless they are the result of recent defoliation. Dieback and dead branches are always excluded from the estimate. Foliage transparency is different from crown density because it emphasizes foliage and ignores stems, branches, fruits, and holes in the crown.

Forest floor. The entire thickness of organic material overlying the mineral soil, consisting of the litter and the duff (humus).

Forest land. Land at least 10 percent stocked by forest trees of any size, or formerly having had such tree cover, and not currently developed for nonforest use. The minimum area considered for classification is 1 acre. Forested strips must be at least 120 feet wide.

Forest management type. A classification of timberland based on forest type and stand origin.

Pine plantation. Stands that (1) have been artificially regenerated by planting or direct seeding, (2) are classed as a pine or other softwood forest type, and (3) have at least 10 percent stocking.

Natural pine. Stands that (1) have not been artificially regenerated, (2) are classed as a pine or other softwood forest type, and (3) have at least 10 percent stocking.

Oak-pine. Stands that have at least 10 percent stocking and classed as a forest type of oak-pine.

Upland hardwood. Stands that have at least 10 percent stocking and classed as an oak-hickory or maple-beech-birch forest type.

Lowland hardwood. Stands that have at least 10 percent stocking with a forest type of oak-gum-cypress, elm-ash-cottonwood, palm, or other tropical.

Nonstocked stands. Stands < 10 percent stocked with live trees.

Forest type. A classification of forest land based on the species forming a plurality of live-tree stocking. Major eastern forest-type groups are:

White-red-jack pine. Forests in which eastern white pine, red pine, or jack pine, singly or in combination, constitute a plurality of the stocking. (Common associates include hemlock, birch, and maple.)

Spruce-fir. Forests in which spruce or true firs, singly or in combination, constitute a plurality of the stocking. (Common associates include maple, birch, and hemlock.)

Longleaf-slash pine. Forests in which longleaf or slash pine, singly or in combination, constitute a plurality of the stocking. (Common associates include oak, hickory, and gum.)

Loblolly-shortleaf pine. Forests in which loblolly pine, shortleaf pine, or other southern yellow pines, except longleaf or slash pine, singly or in combination, constitute a plurality of the stocking. (Common associates include oak, hickory, and gum.)

Oak-pine. Forests in which hardwoods (usually upland oaks) constitute a plurality of the stocking but in which pines account for 25 to 50 percent of the stocking. (Common associates include gum, hickory, and yellow-poplar.)

Oak-hickory. Forests in which upland oaks or hickory, singly or in combination, constitute a plurality of the stocking, except where pines account for 25 to 50 percent, in which case the stand would be classified oak-pine. (Common associates include yellow-poplar, elm, maple, and black walnut.)

Oak-gum-cypress. Bottomland forests in which tupelo, blackgum, sweetgum, oaks, or southern cypress, singly or in combination, constitute a plurality of the stocking, except where pines account for 25 to 50 percent, in which case the stand would be classified oak-pine. (Common associates include cottonwood, willow, ash, elm, hackberry, and maple.)

Elm-ash-cottonwood. Forests in which elm, ash, or cottonwood, singly or in combination, constitute a plurality of the stocking. (Common associates include willow, sycamore, beech, and maple.)

Maple-beech-birch. Forests in which maple, beech, or yellow birch, singly or in combination, constitute a plurality of the stocking. (Common associates include hemlock, elm, basswood, and white pine.)

Nonstocked stands. Stands < 10 percent stocked with live trees.

Forested tract size. The area of forest within the contiguous tract containing each Forest Inventory and Analysis sample plot.

Gross growth. The average annual increase in volume of trees ≥ 5.0 inches d.b.h. in the absence of cutting and mortality. (Gross growth includes survivor growth, ingrowth, growth on ingrowth, growth on removals before removal, and growth on mortality before death.)

Growing-stock trees. Living trees of commercial species classified as sawtimber, poletimber, saplings, and seedlings. Trees must contain at least one 12-foot or two 8-foot logs in the saw-log portion, currently or potentially (if too small to qualify), to be classed as growing stock. The log(s) must meet dimension and merchantability standards to qualify. Trees must also have, currently or potentially, one-third of the gross board-foot volume in sound wood.

Growing-stock volume. The cubic-foot volume of sound wood in growing-stock trees ≥ 5.0 inches d.b.h. from a 1-foot stump to a minimum 4.0-inch top d.o.b. of the central stem.

Hardwoods. Dicotyledonous trees, usually broadleaf and deciduous.

Soft hardwoods. Hardwood species with an average specific gravity of 0.50 or less, such as gums, yellow-poplar, cottonwoods, red maple, basswoods, and willows.

Hard hardwoods. Hardwood species with an average specific gravity > 0.50 such as oaks, hard maples, hickories, and beech.

Hexagonal grid (hex). A hexagonal grid formed from equilateral triangles for the purpose of tessellating the Forest Inventory and Analysis inventory sample. Each hexagon in the base grid has an area of 5,937 acres (2402.6 ha) and contains one inventory plot. The base grid can be subdivided into smaller hexagons to intensify the sample.

Hot check. An inspection normally done as part of the training process. The inspector is present on the plot with the trainee and provides immediate feedback regarding data quality. Data errors are corrected. Hot checks can be done on training plots or production plots. See QA/QC.

Humus. A soil layer dominated by organic material derived from the decomposition of plant and animal litter and deposited on either an organic or a mineral surface. This layer is distinguished from the litter layer in that the original organic material has undergone sufficient decomposition that the source of this material, e.g., individual plant parts, can no longer be identified.

Land area. The area of dry land and land temporarily or partly covered by water, such as marshes, swamps, and river floodplains (omitting tidal flats below mean high tide), streams, sloughs, estuaries, and canals < 200 feet wide, and lakes, reservoirs, and ponds < 4.5 acres in area.

Litter. Undecomposed or only partially decomposed organic material that can be readily identified, e.g., plant leaves, twigs, etc.

Live trees. All living trees. All size classes, all tree classes, and both commercial and noncommercial species are included.

Measurement quality objective (MQO). A data user's estimate of the precision, bias, and completeness of data necessary to satisfy a prescribed application, e.g., Resource Planning Act, assessments by State foresters, forest planning, forest health analyses. Describes the acceptable tolerance for each data element. MQOs consist of two parts: a statement of the tolerance and a percentage of time when the collected data are required to be within tolerance. MQOs can only be assigned where standard methods of sampling or field measurements exist, or where experience has established upper or lower bounds on precision or bias. MQOs can be set for measured data elements, observed data elements, and derived data elements.

Net annual change. The average annual increase or decrease in volume of live trees at least 5.0 inches d.b.h. Net annual change is equal to net annual growth minus average annual removals.

Noncommercial species. Tree species of typically small size, poor form, or inferior quality that normally do not develop into trees suitable for industrial wood products.

Nonforest land. Land that has never supported forests and land formerly forested where timber production is precluded by development for other uses.

Nonstocked stands. Stands < 10 percent stocked with live trees.

Other forest land. Forest land other than timberland and productive reserved forest land. It includes available and reserved forest land which is incapable of producing annually 20 cubic feet per acre of industrial wood under natural conditions, because of adverse site conditions such as sterile soils, dry climate, poor drainage, high elevation, steepness, or rockiness.

Other removals. The growing-stock volume of trees removed from the inventory by cultural operations such as timber stand improvement, land clearing, and other changes in land use, resulting in the removal of the trees from timberland.

Ownership. The property owned by one ownership unit, including all parcels of land in the United States.

National forest land. Federal land that has been legally designated as national forests or purchase units, and other land under the administration of the Forest Service, including experimental areas and Bankhead-Jones Title III land.

Forest industry land. Land owned by companies or individuals operating primary wood-using plants.

Nonindustrial private forest land. Privately owned land excluding forest industry land.

Corporate. Owned by corporations, including incorporated farm ownerships.

Individual. All lands owned by individuals, including farm operators.

Other public. An ownership class that includes all public lands except national forests.

Miscellaneous Federal land. Federal land other than national forests.

State, county, and municipal land. Land owned by States, counties, and local public agencies or municipalities or land leased to these governmental units for ≥ 50 years.

Phase 1 (P1). Forest Inventory and Analysis activities related to remote-sensing, the primary purpose of which is to label plots and obtain stratum weights for population estimates.

Phase 2 (P2). Forest Inventory and Analysis activities conducted on the network of ground plots. The primary purpose is to obtain field data that enable classification and summarization of area, tree, and other attributes associated with forest land uses.

Phase 3 (P3). A subset of phase 2 plots where additional attributes related to forest health are measured.

Poletimber-size trees. Softwoods 5.0 to 8.9 inches d.b.h. and hardwoods 5.0 to 10.9 inches d.b.h.

Productive-reserved forest land. Forest land sufficiently productive to qualify as timberland but withdrawn from timber utilization through statute or administrative regulation.

Quality assurance (QA). The total integrated program for ensuring that the uncertainties inherent in Forest Inventory and Analysis data are known and do not exceed acceptable magnitudes, within a stated level of confidence. QA encompasses the plans, specifications, and policies affecting the collection, processing, and reporting of data. It is the system of activities designed to provide program managers and project leaders with independent assurance that total system QC is being effectively implemented.

Quality control (QC). The routine application of prescribed field and laboratory procedures, e.g., random check cruising, periodic calibration, instrument maintenance, use of certified standards, etc., in order to reduce random and systematic errors and ensure that data are generated within known and acceptable performance limits. QC also ensures the use of qualified personnel; reliable equipment and supplies; training of personnel; good field and laboratory practices; and strict adherence to standard operating procedures.

Reforestation. Area of land previously classified as forest that is regenerated by planting trees or natural regeneration.

Rotten trees. Live trees of commercial species not containing at least one 12-foot saw log, or two noncontiguous saw logs, each ≥ 8 feet, now or prospectively, primarily because of rot or missing sections, and with less than one-third of the gross board-foot tree volume in sound material.

Rough trees. Live trees of commercial species not containing at least one 12-foot saw log, or two noncontiguous saw logs, each ≥ 8 feet, now or prospectively, primarily because of roughness, poor form, splits, and cracks, and with less than one-third of the gross board-foot tree volume in sound material; and live trees of noncommercial species.

Sapling. Live trees 1.0 to 4.9 inches (2.5 to 12.5 cm) in diameter.

Saw log. A log meeting minimum standards of diameter, length, and defect, including logs ≥ 8 feet long, sound and straight, with a minimum diameter inside bark for softwoods of 6 inches (8 inches for hardwoods).

Saw-log portion. The part of the bole of sawtimber trees between a 1-foot stump and the saw-log top.

Saw-log top. The point on the bole of sawtimber trees above which a conventional saw log cannot be produced. The minimum saw-log top is 7.0 inches d.o.b. for softwoods and 9.0 inches d.o.b. for hardwoods.

Sawtimber-size trees. Softwoods ≥ 9.0 inches d.b.h. and hardwoods ≥ 11.0 inches d.b.h.

Sawtimber volume. Growing-stock volume in the saw-log portion of sawtimber-size trees in board feet (International 1/4-inch rule).

Seedlings. Trees < 1.0 inch d.b.h. and > 1 foot tall for hardwoods, > 6 inches tall for softwood, and > 0.5 inch in diameter at ground level for longleaf pine.

Select red oaks. A group of several red oak species composed of cherrybark, Shumard, and northern red oaks. Other red oak species are included in the "other red oaks" group.

Select white oaks. A group of several white oak species composed of white, swamp chestnut, swamp white, chinkapin, Durand, and bur oaks. Other white oak species are included in the "other white oaks" group.

Site class. A classification of forest land in terms of potential capacity to grow crops of industrial wood based on fully stocked natural stands.

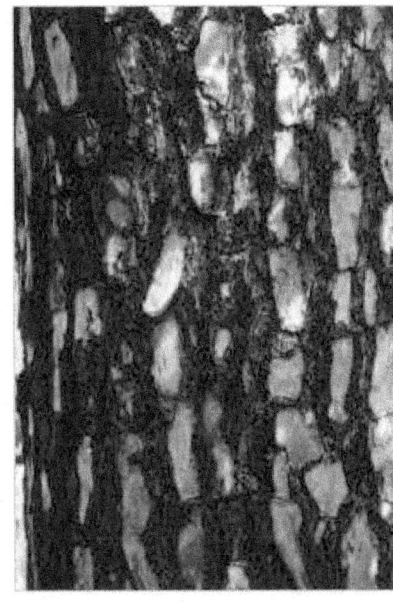

Bark characteristic of mature pine tree. (photo courtesy of the Georgia Forestry Commission)

Softwoods. Coniferous trees, usually evergreen, having leaves that are needles or scalelike.

Yellow pines. Loblolly, longleaf, slash, pond, shortleaf, pitch, Virginia, sand, spruce, and Table Mountain pines.

Other softwoods. Cypress, eastern redcedar, white-cedar, eastern white pine, eastern hemlock, spruce, and fir.

Stand age. The average age of dominant and codominant trees in the stand.

Stand origin. A classification of forest stands describing their means of origin.

Planted. Planted or artificially seeded.

Natural. No evidence of artificial regeneration.

Stand-size class. A classification of forest land based on the diameter class distribution of live trees in the stand.

Sawtimber stands. Stands at least 10 percent stocked with live trees, with one-half or more of total stocking in sawtimber and poletimber trees, and with sawtimber stocking at least equal to poletimber stocking.

Poletimber stands. Stands at least 10 percent stocked with live trees, which one-half or more of total stocking is in poletimber and sawtimber trees, and with poletimber stocking exceeding that of sawtimber.

Sapling-seedling stands. Stands at least 10 percent stocked with live trees of which more than one-half of total stocking is saplings and seedlings.

Nonstocked stands. Stands < 10 percent stocked with live trees.

Stocking. The degree of occupancy of land by trees, measured by basal area or the number of trees in a stand and spacing in the stand, compared with a minimum standard, depending on tree size, required to fully utilize the growth potential of the land.

Density of live trees and basal area per acre required for full stocking:

Timberland. Forest land capable of producing 20 cubic feet of industrial wood per acre per year and not withdrawn from timber utilization.

Tree. Woody plants having one erect perennial stem or trunk ≥ 3 inches d.b.h., a more or less definitely formed crown of foliage, and a height of ≥ 13 feet (at maturity).

Upper-stem portion. The part of the main stem or fork of sawtimber trees above the saw-log top to minimum top diameter 4.0 inches outside bark or to the point where the main stem or fork breaks into limbs.

Volume of live trees. The cubic-foot volume of sound wood in live trees at least 5.0 inches d.b.h. from a 1-foot stump to a minimum 4.0-inch top d.o.b. of the central stem.

Volume of saw-log portion of sawtimber trees. The cubic-foot volume of sound wood in the saw-log portion of sawtimber trees. Volume is the net result after deductions for rot, sweep, and other defects that affect use for lumber.

D.b.h. class	Trees per acre for full stocking	Basal area
inches		*square feet per acre*
Seedlings	600	—
2	560	—
4	460	—
6	340	67
8	240	84
10	155	85
12	115	90
14	90	96
16	72	101
18	60	106
20	51	111

— = not applicable.

Forest Inventory Methods

A State-by-State inventory of the Nation's forest land began in the mid-1930s. These surveys were primarily designed and conducted to provide estimates of forest area, wood volume, tree growth, removals, and mortality. Throughout the years, national concerns over perceived and real trends in forest resource conditions, and numerous technical innovations have led to an array of improvements (Reams and others 2005). The primary purpose for conducting forest inventories has remained unchanged, but the methods have undergone substantial change.

As a reminder of more recent changes in Forest Inventory and Analysis (FIA) survey methodology, a brief discussion of the periodic, variable-radius plot design is included to alert users to substantive changes. These changes necessitate caution in making comparisons with previous forest resource estimates prior to the 1997 survey.

Sample Design Overview: Annual versus Periodic

The 1997 and 2004 surveys' sample design differs in several ways from the one employed in 1989 and previous years. One change involved switching from a periodic survey to an annual survey. Another involved switching from a variable-radius sample to a fixed-plot sample. The plot layouts are different, and, for the most part, plot centers do not overlap. This is a major change that does not allow for tracking plot changes or individual trees from one method to the other. These changes, alone or in combination, weaken comparisons of the last two surveys (1997 and 2004) with the previous surveys. The

only way to quantify the true impact of such changes on trend analysis would be to conduct the survey using both plot designs simultaneously and compare the results of these two independent surveys. Neither the time nor money was available to do this. For the periodic surveys, all plots were measured in about 1 to 2 years, and the time between remeasurements averaged 7 to 10 years. The annual inventory design was implemented to provide the latest information about forest resources updated annually. Under the annual inventory system, 20 percent (one panel) of the total number of plots in a State are measured every year over a 5-year period (one cycle). Each panel of plots is selected on a subgrid which is slightly offset from the previous panel, so that each panel covers essentially the same sample area (both spatially and in intensity) as the prior panel. In the sixth year, the plot data that were measured in

Fall colors on Baker's Mountain, White County, Georgia. (photo courtesy of the Georgia Forestry Commission)

the first panel are dropped and the plots are remeasured and compiled with panels 2 through 5. This marks the beginning of the next cycle of data collection and referred to as the moving average. After field crews have completed remeasurements for all five panels, a new cycle of data is available for the next 5-year report. This dataset consists of data from < 1 year old to 5 years old.

One of the major impacts on data interpretation and analysis of switching to the annual inventory design is the length of time for data collection (5 years, versus 1 or 2 years). Data collected over a longer period of time have a higher probability of sampling a specific event, e.g., a hurricane or fire, but with only a small proportion of the sample. Data collected over a shorter

time span, such as data collected in the periodic survey, however, may miss an event entirely until the next periodic measurement takes place, at which time all of the sample plots reflect the event.

Annual Sample Design

Phase 1–forest area estimates—FIA bases three phases of the current sampling method on a hexagonal grid (hex) design (appendix fig. A.1), with each successive phase sampled with less intensity. There are 27 phase 1 (P1) hexes for every phase 2 (P2) hex and 16 P2 hexes for every phase 3 (P3) hex. P1 hexes represent about 222 acres, while P2 and P3 hexes represent roughly 6,000 and 96,000 acres, respectively.

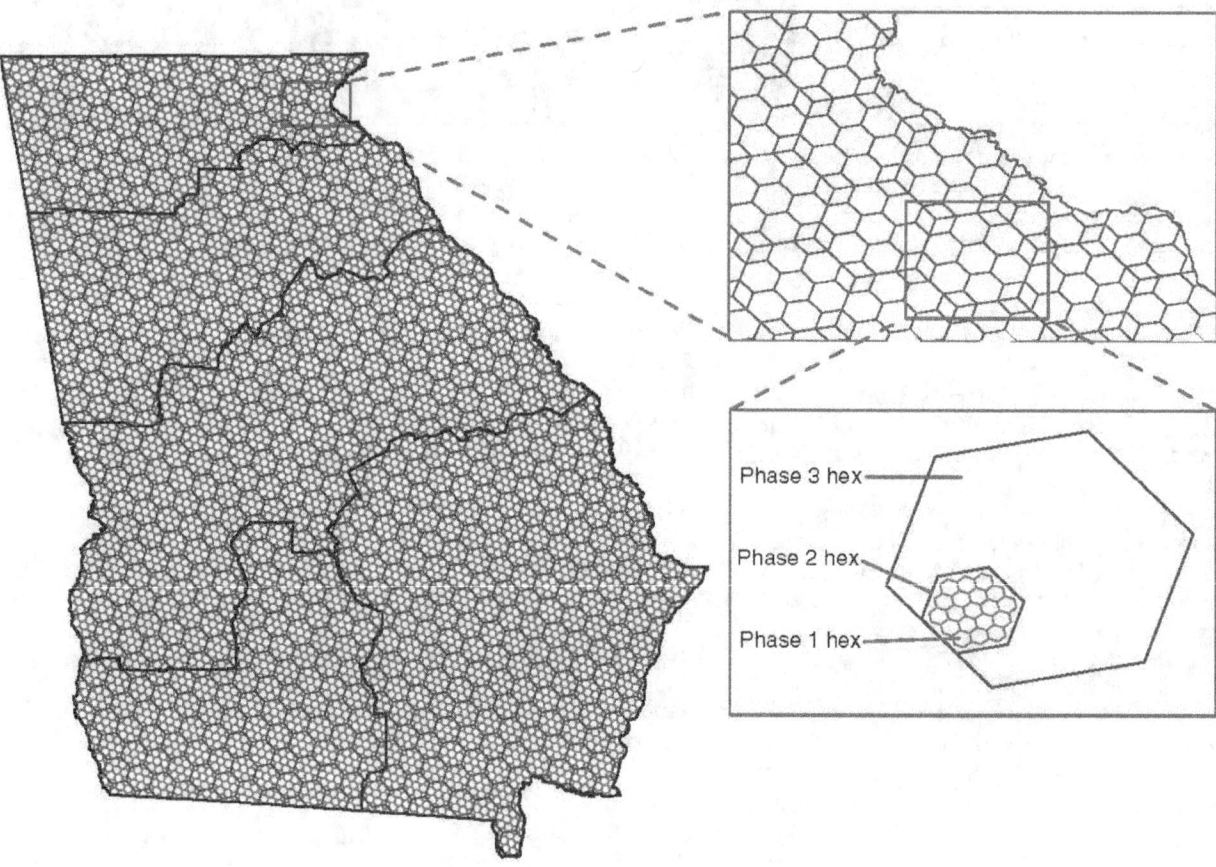

Figure A.1—Depiction of the FIA hexagonal grid (hex) system for location of phase 1, 2, and 3 plots in Georgia.

P1 stratified estimation procedures reduce variance associated with estimates of forest land area and produce more precise estimates than simple random sampling. A statistical estimation technique is used to classify digital satellite imagery and initially stratify the land base as forest or nonforest to assign a representative acreage to each sample plot. Pixels within 60 m (2-pixel widths) of a forest/nonforest boundary formed two additional strata: forest edge and nonforest edge. Forest pixels within 60 m of the boundary on the forest side were classified as forest edge and pixels within 60 m of the boundary on the nonforest side were classified as nonforest edge. The estimated population total for a variable is the sum across all strata of the product of each stratum's area (from the pixel count) and the variable's mean per unit area (from plot measurements) for the stratum. Satellite imagery source data are from 2001 National Land Cover Data (30-m resolution). Recent aerial photography is used to select plots for ground measurement.

P2 locations generally are not placed in the center of the hex. If a sample location from a prior inventory exists in a P2 hex, then that same location is used again. If two sample locations from a prior survey existed within the same hex, then one is dropped. For P2 hexes containing no prior sample location, a new sample location was created at a random point within the hex. This process is performed in a manner that maintains as many existing plots as possible.

Prior to the 2004 Georgia survey, all national forest and public agency forest lands (timberland and reserved), plus forest industry timberland in a county were enumerated. The enumerated or known acreages were taken from public agency reports and other public domain documents at the State and county level.

The 2004 survey does not enumerate public lands. The area assigned to various characteristics (such as ownership, stand size, and forest type) for all area is based on the expansion factor assigned and derived in the first phase. As a result, the published area data by other agencies or entities will likely vary from the 2004 survey data.

Forest Resources: A Global Influence.... (photo by NASA)

Phase 2–forest inventory—Bechtold and Patterson (2005) describe the current P2 and P3 ground plots and explain their use. These plots are clusters of four points arranged so that one point is central and the other three lie 120 feet from it at azimuths of 120, 240, and 360 degrees (fig. A.2). Each point is the center of a circular subplot with a fixed 24-foot radius. Trees ≥ 5.0 inches d.b.h. are measured in these subplots. Each subplot in turn contains a circular microplot with a fixed 6.8-foot radius. Trees 1.0 to 4.9 inches d.b.h. and seedlings (< 1.0 inch d.b.h.) are measured in these microplots.

Sometimes a plot cluster straddles two or more land use or forest condition classes (Bechtold and Patterson 2005). There are seven condition-class variables that require mapping of a unique condition on a plot: (1) land use, (2) forest type, (3) stand size, (4) ownership, (5) stand density, (6) regeneration status, and (7) reserved status. A new condition is defined and mapped each time one of these variables changes during plot measurement.

Phase 3–forest health—Data on forest health variables (P3) are collected on about $1/16^{th}$ of the P2 sample plots. P3 data are coarse descriptions, and are meant to be used as general indicators of overall forest health over large geographic areas. P3 data collection includes variables pertaining to tree crown health, down woody material (DWM), foliar ozone injury, lichen diversity, and soil composition. Tree crown health, DWM, and soil composition measurements are collected using the same plot design used during P2 data collection, while lichen data are collected within a 120-foot-radius circle around the center of each FIA P3 field plot (fig. A.1).

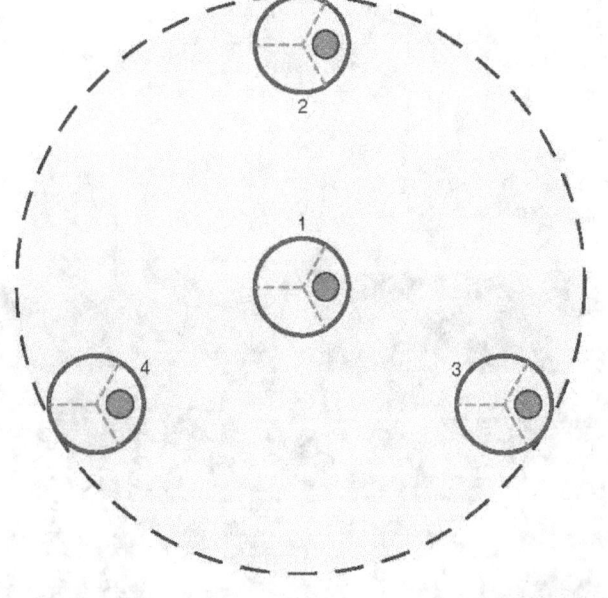

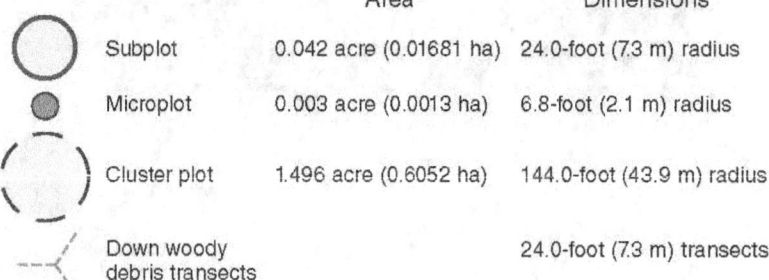

	Area	Dimensions
Subplot	0.042 acre (0.01681 ha)	24.0-foot (7.3 m) radius
Microplot	0.003 acre (0.0013 ha)	6.8-foot (2.1 m) radius
Cluster plot	1.496 acre (0.6052 ha)	144.0-foot (43.9 m) radius
Down woody debris transects		24.0-foot (7.3 m) transects

Figure A.2—Layout of annual fixed-radius plot design. The cluster plot is a circle circumscribing the outer edge of the four subplots.

Biomonitoring sites for ozone data collection are located independently of the FIA grid. Sites must be 1-acre fields or similar open areas adjacent to or surrounded by forest land, and must contain a minimum number of plants of at least two identified bioindicator species (FIA field manual). Plants are evaluated for ozone injury, and voucher specimens are submitted to a regional expert for verification of ozone-induced foliar injury.

Volume Estimation

Tree volumes in Georgia were computed using the simple linear regression model:

$$volume = diameter^2 \times height$$

This equation estimated gross cubic-foot volume from a 1-foot stump to a 4-inch upper diameter for each sample tree. Separate equation coefficients for 77 species or species groupings were utilized. The volume in forks in the central bole and the volume in limbs outside of the main bole were excluded. Net cubic-foot volume was derived by subtracting the estimate of rotten or missing wood for each sample tree. Volume of the saw-log portion (expressed in board feet—International 1/4-inch rule) of sample trees was derived by using board foot-to-cubic foot ratio equations. All equations and coefficients were developed from standing and felled tree volume studies conducted across several Southern States.

Components of Change

A historical feature of FIA inventories allows the measurement of net change over time. Components of change are average annual net growth, removals, and mortality (GRM). The combination of the GRMs provides the average annual net change that occurred during the survey cycle and offers an estimate of whether the forest resource is adding or loosing volume and to what degree.

Forested wetland. (photo courtesy of the Georgia Forestry Commission)

The remeasurement information was used to calculate 11 components of change: (1) survivor growth, (2) ingrowth, (3) growth on ingrowth, (4) reversion, (5) reversion growth, (6) mortality, (7) mortality growth, (8) cut, (9) cut growth, (10) diversions, and (11) diversion growth. This methodology required personnel to account only for previously tallied trees and the history, i.e., survived, died, cut, change in land use. Another change that may have affected estimates of GRM trends was the decrease in the number of plots (plot list change).

GRM estimates were determined from the remeasurement of 5,793 sample plots from the 1997 inventory. This was accomplished by remeasuring trees on the original fixed-radius subplot conditions.

Trees ≥ 5.0 inches d.b.h. in 1997 were remeasured in 2004 on all subplot conditions. Trees that were < 5.0 inches d.b.h. in 1997 and 2004 were remeasured on the microplot. Trees that were < 1.0 inch d.b.h. in 1997 and ≥ 5.0 inches d.b.h. (through-growth trees) in 2004 were measured on the microplots.

For more information, refer to, "The Enhanced Forest Inventory and Analysis Program—National Sampling Design and Estimation Procedures", chapter 4 (Bechtold and Patterson 2005).

Privacy Laws

It is important that forest land owners and FIA data users be aware that Federal law requires that private ownership information collected by FIA shall not be made available for public distribution. In addition, Federal law also requires that the exact locations of all FIA plots shall not be made public so that the ownership of each plot could be determined. This report summarizes FIA data by ownership class at the unit and State level. Breakout of ownership information at the county level for private land is no longer permitted here or on the Forest Inventory and Analysis Database Web site. However, public ownership classes may be summarized at the county level.

Summary

Users wishing to make rigorous comparisons of data between surveys should be aware of the differences in plot designs and variable assessments. Assuming there is no bias in plot selection or maintenance of plot integrity, the most valuable and powerful trend information comes from the same plots being revisited from one survey to the next and measured in the same way. This is also the only method that yields reliable components of change estimation (GRM). This approach lends a higher level of confidence in assessing trends, and reduces variation that is present in forest stands. However, if sample designs change, there can never be a high level of certainty whether trends in the data are real or due to procedural changes. Even though both designs may be judged statistically valid, the naturally occurring variation in the data from one plot design and location to another hinders confident and rigorous assessments of trend over time. Determining the strength of a trend, or determining the level of confidence associated with a trend, is difficult or impossible when sampling methods change over the time period of analysis.

Inventory Quality Assurance and Quality Control

The goal of the FIA quality assurance (QA) program is to provide a framework to assure the production of complete, accurate, and unbiased forest assessments for given standards. One of the goals of the FIA Program is to include data quality documentation in all nationally available reports including State reports and national summary reports. This report includes a summary of P2 variables and measurement quality objective (MQO) analyses from FIA blind check measurements. Quality assessments of the P3 data will be addressed in future reports. Quality control (QC) procedures include feedback to field staff to provide assessment and improvement of crew performance. Additionally, data quality is assessed and documented using performance measurements and postsurvey assessments. These assessments are then used to identify areas of the data collection process that need improvement or refinement in order to meet quality objectives of the program.

Quality Assurance and Quality Control Methods

FIA implements QA methods in several different ways. These methods include nationally standardized field manuals, portable data recorders (PDR), training and certification of field crews, and field audits. The PDRs help assure that specified procedures are followed. The minimum national standards for annual training of field crews are: (1) a minimum of 40 hours for new employees and (2) a minimum of 8 hours for return employees. Field crew members are certified via an in-situ test plot. All crews are required to have at least one certified person present on the plot at all times.

Data collection crew. (SRS photo)

Field Audits

Hot check—A hot check is an inspection normally done as part of the training process. The inspector is present with crew to document crew performance as they measure plots. The recommended intensity for hot checks is 2 percent of the plots installed.

Cold check—A cold check is done at regular intervals throughout the field season. The crew that installed the plot is not present at the time of inspection and does not know when or which plots will be remeasured. The inspector visits the completed plot, evaluates the crew's data collection, and notes corrections where necessary. The recommended intensity for cold checks is 5 percent of the plots installed.

Blind check—A blind check is a complete reinstallation measurement of a previously completed plot. However, the QA crew remeasurement is done without the previously recorded data. The first measurement of the plot is referred to as the field measurement and the second measurement as the QA measurement. The field crews do not know in advance when or which of their plots will be measured by a QA crew. This type of blind measurement provides a direct, unbiased observation of measurement precision from two independent crews. Plots selected for blind checks are chosen to be a representative subsample of all plots measured and are randomly selected. Blind checks are planned to be within a 2-week window of the field measurement. The recommended intensity for blind checks is 3 percent of the plots installed.

Measurement Quality Objectives

Each variable collected by FIA is assigned a MQO with desired levels of tolerance for data analyses. The MQOs are documented in the FIA national field manual (U.S. Department of Agriculture 2004a, 2004b). In some instances the MQOs were established as a "best guess" of what experienced field crews should be able to consistently achieve. Tolerances are somewhat arbitrary and were based on the ability of crews to make repeatable measurements or observations within the assigned MQO. Evaluation of field crew

performance is accomplished by calculation of the differences between the field crew and QA crew data collected on blind check plots. Results of these calculations are compared to the established MQOs.

In the analysis of blind check data, an observation is within tolerance when the difference between the field crew and QA crew observations do not exceed the assigned tolerance for that variable. For many categorical variables, the tolerance is "no error" allowed, thus only observations that are identical are within the tolerance level.

Georgia was the first State to begin the annual inventory and underwent extensive change regarding the cataloguing QA/QC records. Only one panel of QA/QC data is available for analysis and is not included. For more information, please contact the author at the Knoxville, TN, office.

Sampling Error

Sampling error is associated with the natural and expected deviation of the sample from the true population mean. This deviation is susceptible to a mathematical evaluation of the probability of error. Sampling errors for State totals are based on one standard deviation. That is, there is a 68.27-percent probability that the confidence interval given for each sample estimate will cover the true population mean (table B.1)

The size of the sampling error generally increases as the size of the area examined decreases. Also, as area or volume totals are stratified by forest type, species,

diameter class, ownership, or other subunits, the sampling error may increase and be greatest for the smallest divisions. However, there may be instances where a smaller component does not have a proportionately larger sampling error. This can happen when the postdefined strata are more homogeneous than the larger strata, thereby having a smaller variance. For specific postdefined strata the sampling error is available from online retrievals using the Forest Inventory Data Online at: "http://199.128.173.26/fido/mastf/index.html" or can be calculated using the following formula. Sampling errors obtained by this method are only approximations of reliability because this process assumes constant variance across all subdivisions of totals.

$$SE_s = SE_t \frac{\sqrt{X_t}}{\sqrt{X_s}}$$

where

SE_s = sampling error for subdivision of State total

SE_t = sampling error for State total

X_s = sum of values for the variable of interest (area or volume) for subdivision of State

X_t = total area or volume for State

For example, the estimate of sampling error for area of longleaf pine forest type on all timberland is computed as:

$$SE_s = 0.54 \frac{\sqrt{24246.5}}{\sqrt{463.5}} = 3.91$$

Thus, the sampling error is 3.91 percent, and the resulting 67-percent confidence interval for longleaf forest type on all timberland is 463.5 thousand acres ± 18.1 thousand acres.

Table B.1—Statistical reliability for Georgia, 2004

Item	Sample estimate and confidence interval		Sampling error
			percent
Timberland (*1,000 acres*)	24,246.5 ±	130.9	0.54
All live (*million cubic feet*)			
Inventory	36,577.2 ±	464.5	1.27
Net annual growth	2,022.7 ±	45.3	2.24
Annual removals	1,614.2 ±	81.2	5.03
Annual mortality	38.8 ±	1.4	3.59
Growing stock (*million cubic feet*)			
Inventory	33,051.4 ±	439.6	1.33
Net annual growth	1,923.9 ±	42.9	2.23
Annual removals	1,574.4 ±	79.7	5.06
Annual mortality	292.2 ±	18.6	6.38
Sawtimber (*million board feet*[a])			
Inventory	106,655.0 ±	2,015.8	1.89
Net annual growth	6,035.7 ±	189.5	3.14
Annual removals	4,995.5 ±	292.2	5.85
Annual mortality	1,024.2 ±	102.1	9.97

[a] International ¼-inch rule.

The Flint River from Sprewell Bluff looking at Upson and Talbot Counties Georgia. (photo courtesy of the Georgia Forestry Commission)

Mature pine stand in South Georgia. (photo courtesy of the Georgia Forestry Commission)

Timber Product Inventory

Estimates of timber product output (TPO) and plant residues were obtained from canvasses (questionnaires) sent to all primary wood-using mills in the State. The canvasses are used to determine the types and amount of roundwood, i.e., saw logs, pulpwood, poles, etc., received by each mill, the county of origin of the wood, the species used, and how the mills dispose of the bark and wood residues produced. The canvasses are conducted every 2 years by personnel by the Georgia Forestry Commission and the Southern Research Station. These data are used to augment FIA's annual inventory of timber removals by providing the product proportions for that segment of removals that is used for products. Individual studies are necessary to track trends and changes in product output levels. Industry surveys conducted in 1997, 1999, 2001, and 2003 were used to determine average annual product output for roundwood and plant byproducts. Total

product output, averaged over the survey period, is the sum of the volume of roundwood products from all sources (growing stock and other sources) and the volume of plant byproducts, or the mill residues.

The TPO database can be accessed from the Forest Service, Southern Research Station, Forest Inventory and Analysis Web site at: http://srsfia2.fs.fed.us/.

National Woodland Owner Survey

FIA conducted a questionnaire survey, formally known as the National Woodland Owner Survey, to obtain information about the family forest owner group (www.fs.fed. us/nwos). Questionnaires were sent to a sample of private forest land owners in Georgia during 2002 to 2004. By design, the sample excluded landowners who own no forest land. The tables for families or individuals owning 10 or more acres of timberland were chosen for this report because 68 percent of the families or individuals in Georgia own < 10 acres. This represented < 8 percent of the timberland area. This disparity of the large number of ownerships to the total acres of timberland appeared to have some influence on certain questions when included. A total of 643 survey responses by owners of 10 or more acres were returned by Georgia landowners for the 2004 survey between 2002 and 2004 (table B.2). Responses by mail accounted for about 77 percent of all survey responses. The remaining 23 percent were telephone respondents.

Table B.2—National Woodland Owner Survey sample sizes for family forest owners in Georgia (10+ acres), 2002 to 2004

Response type						
Mail			Telephone			Total
2002	2003	2004	2002	2003	2004	responses
222	169	104	36	73	39	643

Species List[a]

Common name	Scientific name[b]	Common name	Scientific name[b]
Softwoods		Hardwoods (continued)	
Atlantic white-cedar	*Chamaecyparis thyoides*	Red hickory	*C. glabra* var. *ordorata*
Southern redcedar	*Juniperus silicicola*	Pecan	*C. illinoensis*
Eastern redcedar	*J. virginiana*	Shellbark hickory	*C. laciniosa*
Sand pine	*Pinus clausa*	Nutmeg hickory	*C. myristiciformis*
Shortleaf pine	*P. echinata*	Shagbark hickory	*C. ovata*
Slash pine	*P. elliottii*	Sand hickory	*C. pallida*
Spruce pine	*P. glabra*	Black hickory	*C. texana*
Longleaf pine	*P. palustris*	Mockernut hickory	*C. tomentosa*
Table Mountain pine	*P. pungens*	American chestnut	*Castanea dentata*
Pitch pine	*P. rigida*	Catalpa	*Catalpa* spp.
Pond pine	*P. serotina*	Southern catalpa	*C. bignonioides*
Eastern white pine	*P. strobus*	Sugarberry	*Celtis laevigata*
Loblolly pine	*P. taeda*	Hackberry	*C. occidentalis*
Virginia pine	*P. virginiana*	Eastern redbud	*Cercis canadensis*
Baldcypress	*Taxodium distichum*	Flowering dogwood	*Cornus florida*
Pondcypress	*T. distichum* var. *nutans*	Hawthorn	*Crataegus* spp.
Hemlock	*Tsuga* spp.	Cockspur hawthorn	*C. crus-galli*
Eastern hemlock	*T. canadensis*	Downy hawthorn	*C. mollis*
Carolina hemlock	*T. caroliniana*	Common persimmon	*Diospyros virginiana*
Hardwoods		American beech	*Fagus grandifolia*
Florida maple	*Acer barbatum*	Other palms	*Family Arecaceae not listed above*
Chalk maple	*A. leucoderme*		
Boxelder	*A. negundo*	Ash	*Fraxinus* spp.
Black maple	*A. nigrum*	White ash	*F. americana*
Striped maple	*A. pensylvanicum*	Carolina ash	*F. caroliniana*
Red maple	*A. rubrum*	Green ash	*F. pennsylvanica*
Silver maple	*A. saccharinum*	Waterlocust	*Gleditsia aquatica*
Sugar maple	*A. saccharum*	Honeylocust	*G. triacanthos*
Mountain maple	*A. spicatum*	Loblolly-bay	*Gordonia lasianthus*
Yellow buckeye	*Aesculus flava*	Silverbell	*Halesia* spp.
Ohio buckeye	*A. glabra*	Carolina silverbell	*H. carolina*
Ailanthus	*Ailanthus altissima*	American holly	*Ilex opaca*
Mimosa, silktree	*Albizia julibrissin*	Butternut	*Juglans cinerea*
Serviceberry	*Amelanchier* spp.	Black walnut	*J. nigra*
Birch	*Betula* spp.	Sweetgum	*Liquidambar styraciflua*
Yellow birch	*B. alleghaniensis*	Yellow-poplar	*Liriodendron tulipifera*
Sweet birch	*B. lenta*	Osage-orange	*Maclura pomifera*
River birch	*B. nigra*	Cucumbertree	*Magnolia acuminata*
American hornbeam, musclewood	*Carpinus caroliniana*	Mountain or Fraser magnolia	*M. fraseri*
		Southern magnolia	*M. grandiflora*
Hickory	*Carya* spp.	Bigleaf magnolia	*M. macrophylla*
Water hickory	*C. aquatica*	Sweetbay	*M. virginiana*
Bitternut hickory	*C. cordiformis*	Apple	*Malus* spp.
Pignut hickory	*C. glabra*		

continued

Species List[a] (continued)

Common name	Scientific name[b]	Common name	Scientific name[b]
Hardwoods (continued)		Hardwoods (continued)	
Southern crab apple	*M. angustifolia*	Overcup oak	*Q. lyrata*
Chinaberry	*Melia azedarach*	Blackjack oak	*Q. marilandica*
Mulberry	*Morus* spp.	Swamp chestnut oak	*Q. michauxii*
White mulberry	*M. alba*	Chinkapin oak	*Q. muehlenbergii*
Red mulberry	*M. rubra*	Water oak	*Q. nigra*
Water tupelo	*Nyssa aquatica*	Willow oak	*Q. phellos*
Ogeechee tupelo	*N. ogeche*	Chestnut oak	*Q. prinus*
Swamp tupelo, blackgum	*N. sylvatica* var. *biflora*	Northern red oak	*Q. rubra*
Eastern hophornbeam	*Ostrya virginiana*	Shumard oak	*Q. shumardii*
Sourwood	*Oxydendrum arboreum*	Post oak	*Q. stellata*
Paulownia, empress-tree	*Paulownia tomentosa*	Dwarf post oak	*Q. stellata* var. *margaretta*
Redbay	*Persea borbonia*	Delta post oak	*Q. stellata* var. *paludosa*
Water-elm planetree	*Planera aquatica*	Black oak	*Q. velutina*
American Sycamore	*Platanus occidentalis*	Live oak	*Q. virginiana*
Cottonwood and poplar	*Populus* spp.	Dwarf live oak	*Q. virginiana* var. *minima*
Eastern cottonwood	*P. deltoides*	Black locust	*Robinia pseudoacacia*
Cherry and plum	*Prunus* spp.	Cabbage palmetto	*Sabal palmetto*
American plum	*P. americana*	Willow	*Salix* spp.
Pin cherry	*P. pensylvanica*	Black willow	*S. nigra*
Black cherry	*P. serotina*	Chinese tallowtree	*Sapium sebiferum*
Chokecherry	*P. virginiana*	Sassafras	*Sassafras albidum*
Oak deciduous	*Quercus* spp.	American basswood	*Tilia americana*
White oak	*Q. alba*	White basswood	*T. heterophylla*
Swamp white oak	*Q. bicolor*	Unknown hardwood	*Tree, broadleaf*
Scarlet oak	*Q. coccinea*	Elm	*Ulmus* spp.
Durand oak	*Q. durandii*	Winged elm	*U. alata*
Southern red oak	*Q. falcata*	American elm	*U. americana*
Cherrybark oak	*Q. falcata* var. *pagodifolia*	Cedar elm	*U. crassifolia*
Scrub oak	*Q. ilicifolia*	Siberian elm	*U. pumila*
Bluejack oak	*Q. incana*	Slippery elm	*U. rubra*
Turkey oak	*Q. laevis*	September elm	*U. serotina*
Laurel oak	*Q. laurifolia*		

[a] Only trees ≥ 1.0 inch d.b.h. occurring in the FIA sample.
[b] Little (1979).

Harper, Richard A.; McClure, Nathan D.; Johnson, Tony G. [and others]. 2009. Georgia's forests, 2004. Resour. Bull. SRS–149. Asheville, NC: U.S. Department of Agriculture Forest Service, Southern Research Station.

Between 1997 and 2004, the Forest Service, Forest Inventory and Analysis Program conducted the eighth inventory of Georgia forests. Forest land area remained stable at 24.8 million acres, and covered about two-thirds of the land area in Georgia. About 24.2 million acres of forest land was considered timberland and 92 percent of that was privately owned. Family forest ownership accounted for 14.3 million acres of the timberland and represented 168,000 landowners with 10 or more acres of timberland. Forest industry ownership, with 4.3 million acres, continued to decline and corporate ownership increased to 3.8 million acres. Loblolly pine remained the predominant softwood forest type and occupied 6.8 million acres. Restoration efforts increased longleaf pine area by 23 percent since 1997. Planted pine accounted for 6.5 million acres and natural pine occupied 4.3 million acres. Hardwood forest types slightly overshadowed softwood with 55 percent of the timberland area. Softwood volume for all live trees reached an alltime high of 17.7 billion cubic feet. Hardwood volume for live trees also reached an alltime high of 18.9 billion cubic feet. Volume for all live trees in pine plantations rose sharply and marked a 45-percent increase to 6.7 billion cubic feet since 1997. Net annual growth for all live softwoods increased 36 percent and averaged 1.4 billion cubic feet per year since 1997. During this same period, hardwood net annual growth increased 14 percent and averaged 0.6 billion cubic feet per year. Net annual growth outpaced removals by 21 percent for softwoods and almost 38 percent for hardwoods.

Keywords: Annual inventory, economic impact, FIA, forest health, forest ownership, nontimber forest products, timber product output.

The Forest Service, U.S. Department of Agriculture (USDA), is dedicated to the principle of multiple use management of the Nation's forest resources for sustained yields of wood, water, forage, wildlife, and recreation. Through forestry research, cooperation with the States and private forest owners, and management of the National Forests and National Grasslands, it strives—as directed by Congress—to provide increasingly greater service to a growing Nation.

June 2009

Southern Research Station
200 W.T. Weaver Blvd.
Asheville, NC 28804

Georgia: The Peach State

Capital City: Atlanta

Location: 33.762 N., 84.422 W.

Origin of State's Name: Named for King George II of England

Nickname: Peach State, Empire of the South

Population: 9,544,750 (2007 estimate)

Largest City: Atlanta

Geology:
  Land Area: 57,906 square miles; 24th largest State
  Inland Water: 1,518 square miles
  Coastline: 100 miles
  Highest Point: Brasstown Bald; 4,784 feet
  Lowest Point: Alantic coast; sea level

Border States: Alabama, Florida, North Carolina, South Carolina, Tennessee

Constitution: 4th State

Statehood: January 2, 1788

Agriculture: Poultry and eggs, peanuts, cattle, hogs, dairy products, vegetables

Industry: Textiles and apparel, transportation equipment, food processing, paper products, chemical products, electric equipment, tourism

Natural Resources: Georgia's natural resources include a variety of mineral deposits (clays, large granite deposits, marble, feldspar, some gold, barite, manganese, bauxite, fuller's earth, kaolin, bentonites, coal, kyanite, limestone, mica), great forests, and abundant water supplies.

Bird: Brown Thrasher—On April 6, 1935, the brown thrasher was first chosen as the Georgia state bird by official proclamation of the Governor. In 1970, at the request of the Garden Clubs of Georgia, it was designated by the legislature as the official State bird. The thrasher is commonly found in the eastern section of the United States, ranging north to Canada and west to the Rockies. The bird migrates to the North in the summer and spends its winters in the Southern states. Almost a foot in length, the thrasher has a long, curved bill and a very long tail. It has two prominent white wing bars, a rich brown color on its top side, and a creamy white breast heavily streaked with brown.

Tree: In 1937, the live oak was adopted as the official tree at the request of the Edmund Burke Chapter of the Daughters of the American Revolution. It flourishes along the Coastal Plains and on the islands where the first settlers made their homes. Many famous Georgians, as early as General James Edward Oglethorpe, were able to enjoy its beauty.

Flower: Cherokee rose—In 1916, with the support of the Georgia Federation of Women's Clubs, the Cherokee rose was named the State floral emblem. The name "Cherokee Rose" is a local designation derived from the Cherokee Indians who widely distributed the plant. The rose is excessively thorny and generously supplied with leaves of a vivid green. In color, it is waxy white with a large golden center. Blooming time is in the early spring, but favorable conditions will produce, in the fall of the year, a second flowering of this hardy plant.

Song: On April 24, 1979, the song "Georgia On My Mind," with music by Hoagy Carmichael and lyrics by Stuart Gorrell, was designated Georgia's official State song. It was performed on March 7, 1979, before a joint meeting of the Georgia Senate and House of Representatives by Georgia-born recording artist Ray Charles.

Presidental Birthplace: James Earl Carter, Jr., 39th President

Flag: Georgia designated a new State flag in 2003. Based on the national flag of the Confederacy, it has three bars of equal width—two outer red bars and a center white. There is a square blue canton the width of two bars in the upper left corner. Georgia's coat of arms is centered on the canton with the words "In God We Trust" below (both in gold). Circling the coat of arms are 13 white stars, symbols of Georgia and the other 12 original States that formed the United States of America.

Seal: The State seal of Georgia was adopted by the State Constitution in 1798. The obverse (main face) features the State coat of arms. The three pillars are symbols of the legislative, judicial, and executive branches of government. The man standing with drawn sword defends the constitution and its principles of wisdom, justice, and moderation.

Motto: "Wisdom, Justice & Moderation"

Information courtesy of: "http://www.infoplease. com", "http://www.50states.com", "http://www. statesymbolsusa.org", http://www.netstate.com.